ENGLISH HERITAGE

CONTENTS

Mike Corbishley

Mike Corbishley

English Heritage Education Service

ABOUT THIS BOOK

Most places have at least one church or chapel. Towns usually contain a number. Locally accessible, these buildings, their sites and surroundings, offer practical and analytical learning opportunities, not only for history and religious education, but also for maths, science, technology, geography, art - and links between them.

'Church' is a word with two senses: a body of believers ('the Christian Church') and a building where believers meet for worship. This book is about the buildings, but it is important for pupils to be reminded that Church members regard their buildings as expressions of living faith, not inert monuments. Like history itself, a church is not a finished or 'given' artefact, but something dynamic, still in process of change.

This book aims to:

■ equip teachers with information that sets places of worship in their religious, historical and social contexts

■ explore interdisciplinary links

■ offer ideas for study, projects, and follow-up work.

Cathedrals are used to receiving large numbers of visitors who wish to explore the building. Some cathedrals have materials specifically produced for teachers and their pupils. However, most churches and chapels are unused to groups of people visiting for educational purposes. Most, of course, are still used for worship and attract the loyalties and affections of local people, whose relatives may be buried there. Members of the congregation are usually pleased to see their church as a focus for lively interest, but some may resent any suggestion, even if unintended, that their building is merely an ancient monument. As with any resource, you should visit in advance to find out who to contact and how best to fit in with services and meetings.

ABOVE: St. Marks Church, North Audley Street, London, built in 1824-8 with a neo-Greek front.
TOP RIGHT: Lindisfarne Holy Island was founded in AD 635. The priory church seen here dates from the twelfth century.
BELOW TO RIGHT: A Church of England chapel for the villagers of Stones Green, an outlying hamlet of a large parish in Essex. This chapel, built of wood and corrugated iron, replaced a stone building in about 1929.
RIGHT: St Swithuns Church, Compton Beauchamp, Oxfordshire.
BELOW: Ely Cathedral. This view of the east end shows the thirteenth-century chancel, enlarged from the Norman original. On the right is the Lady Chapel, built c1335-1353.

TIMELINE

300+ By the early fourth century AD there are churches in Roman Britain.

432 Patrick evangelises in Ireland. The length of Patrick's missionary work is uncertain: 432 is its traditional starting date.

c 563 Religious community founded at Iona.

596 Augustine and a group of monks are despatched from Rome by pope Gregory I to convert Ethelbert, king of Kent. By 579 Ethelbert had married Bertha, a Frankish princess, who was already a Christian.

597 Augustine and his missioners reach Kent. Ethelbert welcomes them, and in following years they build or restore several churches in and around Canterbury.

604 Episcopal sees established in London and Rochester.

668 Theodore, a monk from Asia Minor, is appointed to the see of Canterbury. He arrives in England in 669, and during the 670s and 680s establishes an expanded network of dioceses.

674 Benedict Biscop (an English nobleman) establishes a religious community and church at Monkwearmouth, followed by a second church at nearby Jarrow in 681.

731 Bede completes his Ecclesiastical History. During the first half of the 8th century literary activity, the arts and architecture flourish. Missionary activity is carried from England into Germany.

793 Lindisfarne is raided by the Danes.

900+ Churches for the use of local, secular populations are founded in increasing numbers during the 10th and 11th centuries.

c 1050 The Romanesque style, already adopted in some progressive monastic and cathedral churches, begins to make its appearance in parish churches.

1066 Norman Conquest. During the next fifty years almost all existing cathedrals, churches of religious communities, and a majority of parish churches are rebuilt in the Romanesque style, with a new sense of scale.

1078 Legates are sent from Rome to reorganise the English Church.

1086 Domesday Survey.

1093 Work begins on a new cathedral at Durham. Technologically advanced, its spaces are to be covered by the first surviving system of ribbed vaults in Europe.

c 1175 Early English Gothic, which takes the pointed arch as a leading theme, begins to displace the Romanesque style.

1st-10th Centuries	11th Century	12th Century	13th Century	14th Century
1000	**1100**	**1200**	**1300**	**1400**

627 A church is built in York, in which Edwin, king of Northumbria, is baptised by Paulinus, a Roman missionary.

632 Edwin is killed in battle by Penda (pagan king of Mercia) and his ally Cadwallon (the Christian king of Gwynedd).

634-5 Oswald, Edwin's effective successor as king of Northumbria, invites Irish monks at Iona to send a mission to his kingdom. They establish a religious community on Lindisfarne.

661+ Wilfrid oversees the construction of a monastic church at Ripon, the crypt of which survives beneath the present (later) cathedral. A crypt of broadly similar character and date, also of Wilfridian origin, exists under the church at Hexham.

664 Disagreement between churchmen of Irish and Roman tendency on such matters as the correct method of calculating Easter is settled, in favour of Rome, at the Synod of Whitby.

c 800-900 Monastic communities and dioceses in much of northern and eastern England are weakened by Danish incursions - initially by looting, but subsequently and probably more fundamentally by seizure of their estates and the displacement of supportive local leaders. King Alfred (871-99) laments the decline, but church building and renovation continue.

970 A conference held in Winchester heralds fresh efforts to reform monastic and ecclesiastical life. A number of religious communities are reformed or refounded in following years.

1200 Almost all medieval parish churches are now standing.

c 1250 First essays in Decorated style, which employs bar tracery (permitting much enlarged and ornate windows) and delights in embellishment and sinuous patterns.

1320+ First inventions in Perpendicular - a wholly English style - begin to appear. From around 1350 until the Tudor age Perpendicular holds sway.

1380 John Wycliffe translates the Bible into English.

Colchester Archaeological Trust/Peter Froste

RIGHT: This is an artist's impression of a Christian church built in Colchester between AD 320 and 340 and remained in use until least AD 400. Its remains were excavated by the Colchester Archaeological Trust.

1529-40 Henry VIII reforms Parliament and dissolves monasteries. The Church of England is formed with the monarch as its head.

1545-7 Dissolution of chantries.
by 1550 Some congregations gather to hear the Word of the Lord apart from the Church of England. Many such Separatists eventually become Congregationalists (or the Independency).

1554-58 Brief Catholic restoration under Mary Tudor.

1559 Elizabeth I re-establishes authority of the monarch over the English Church.

1609 John Smyth begins to baptise adult believers.

1643 Presbyterian Assembly of Divines.

1652 Large increase in membership of Society of Friends.

1711 Parliament establishes a Commission for Building Fifty New Churches in London. When the Commission's work ceases in 1733 the total of completed projects is 19.

1729 The Wesley brothers and others form a Holy Club in Oxford. For their methodical devotion they are nicknamed 'methodists'.

1744 First annual Methodist general conference.

1784 Methodist societies are given legal status. Some 356 chapels now exist in England and Wales.

1791 John Wesley dies. There are now some 100,000 Methodists.

1791 Relief Act legalises the building of Roman Catholic churches.

1817 First edition of Thomas Rickman's *Attempt to Discriminate the Styles of English Architecture*: one of the earliest successful attempts to establish a reliable typological framework for medieval architecture, and which coins the stylistic names of Early English, Decorated and Perpendicular.

1818 Church Building Act establishes a Commission for 'building and promoting the building of additional churches in populous parishes'.

1832 Congregational Union of England and Wales.

1832 Parliament approves a Bill for establishing a 'General Cemetery' in the vicinity of London. Kensal Green garden cemetery opens in 1833. Others follow at Norwood (1837), Highgate (1839), Abney Park (1840) and elsewhere.

1839 Formation of Cambridge Camden Society, which by 1844 argues that the Decorated style was the architecture more perfectly matched to Christian doctrine than any other, and urges the restoration of existing churches and the building of new ones accordingly.

...tury	16th Century	17th Century	18th Century	19th Century	20th Century
1500	**1600**	**1700**	**1800**	**1900**	

1662 Following the Act of Uniformity, some 2,000 ministers refuse to subscribe, secede from the Church of England and form Presbyterian churches.

1687 Declaration of Indulgence, which allows Roman Catholic and nonconformist worship.

1689 Act of Toleration exempts Protestant dissenters (except Unitarians) from some penal laws and guarantees their freedom of worship. From now on nonconformist places of worship and meeting are built, and survive, in increasing numbers.

Window in 'Albion Chapel', Ashton-under-Lyne, Lancashire, built 1890-5 in a Late Gothic idiom for the Congregational (now United Reform) Church. The glass is of outstanding quality, and here shows scenes from the life of the Roman emperor Constantine, who made a pilgrimage to the Holy Places.

1843 John Claudius Loudon publishes his influential treatise *On the laying out, planting, and managing of Cemeteries*.

1849 John Ruskin describes 'restoration' as 'destruction accompanied with a false description of the thing destroyed'.

1856 Work of the Church Building Commission ends. 612 new churches have been erected.

1877 William Morris and others found the Society for the Protection of Ancient Buildings. Hostile to restoration, their doctrine of conservative repair will be the foundation of 20th-century conservation philosophy.

1914 Dibdin Commission is established to examine the Church of England's system for the care of parish churches. The strategy it recommends - a network of Diocesan Advisory Committees - forms the basis of Anglican conservation care today.

1972 United Reformed Church is founded by union of Congregationalists and Presbyterians.

The imagery on eighteenth-century memorials is often concerned with mortality (skull and crossed bones, the tools of the sexton, the hourglass, sundial and candle) especially in the early part of the century.

DEFINITIONS AND SETTINGS

CHURCHES

'Church' can refer to all kinds of building, but for present purposes the word is limited to parish churches. A parish is a local unit of pastoral care. Parish churches are places for rites of passage - baptism, marriage, burial - and regular devotion. Together with their surrounding spaces they are also places of communal life and meeting.

CATHEDRALS, ABBEYS AND PRIORIES

Cathedrals are usually imagined as big and special churches. Many of them are, but neither size nor architectural form actually define a cathedral, which is properly the principal church of a bishop's diocese. The bishop's authority is symbolised by his *cathedra*: a throne or chair. Move the chair to another church, and you move the cathedral. The diocese of Bath and Wells, for instance, is so called because at different times the cathedra stood in both. During the last 150 years a number of large parish churches in growing industrial towns like Bradford, Coventry and Sheffield were promoted to cathedral status.

For archaeological purposes cathedrals, abbeys and priories can usually be regarded as a single category, conveniently thought of as 'great churches'. Bear in mind that cathedrals remain in active use, whereas most monastic churches are either in ruins (often in the care of English Heritage) or have disappeared since the Reformation.

Many of our great churches originated before the Norman Conquest, some in the missionary age of the seventh and eighth centuries when England was converted to Christianity by bishops, holy men and women from Italy, Frankish Gaul, and Ireland. A number were rebuilt and enlarged in the ninth-eleventh centuries. Few traces of these enterprises are to be seen above ground – Norman rebuilding was near-comprehensive

Vertical photograph of the Anglo-Saxon cathedral at Canterbury, partially excavated in advance of reflooring in 1992-93.

Canterbury Archaeological Trust

although archaeological excavations give us glimpses of what they were like.

A few great churches, like the abbey churches at Tewkesbury Abbey or Romsey, were taken over by local communities after 1540, and survive in use as large parish churches.

What were great churches for?

Cathedral and monastic churches were for the use of religious communities: men or women who lived a life in common, according to a formal regime or rule. Such churches were therefore parts of larger groups of buildings where the canons, monks or nuns lived, ate and slept. These functions in their turn required further buildings for the processing of food, craft working, care of the sick and

RIGHT: Cadaver tomb in Tewkesbury Abbey. Such grisly memorials appear in the fifteenth century, reminding us of the late medieval preoccupation not only with mutability, but also with the need for the living to provide spiritual support for the dead. In this sense, 'society' in the medieval period was trans-temporal, embracing all Christians, whether alive or departed.

elderly, and the reception of guests.

In an age before the Welfare State religious communities also specialised in providing charity for the elderly, displaced or sick. Their actions thereby reflected well upon the patrons who provided the resources.

Great churches were sponsored by royalty or aristocracy, who enabled religious communities to exist by providing sites for their monasteries, and land (which yielded agricultural produce that could be converted to income) in return for prayers.

A cathedral community or great church can thus be seen as representing a bargain between the patron(s) who made it possible, and the priests, monks or nuns who formed its community. A patron expected to have an easier time it in Purgatory because of the masses said by the community (s)he had founded.

All great churches were prayer factories, but cathedrals had extra functions as the churches of bishops who exercised pastoral supervision over the parish churches and priests in their dioceses. Cathedrals were thus accompanied by a number of other specialised buildings,

Council for British Archaeology

such as a palace for the bishop, grand houses for the leaders of the cathedral community, and a chapter house - a religious conference room - where the community could meet. The senior members of the community ranked as noblemen, and each of their houses would be something like a complete manorial complex, with facilities for visitors, servants, storage of produce, and stables.

Cathedral size

Why are some cathedrals so large? Why, for instance, are the naves of abbeys like St Albans or Ely so long? Were they meant to hold lots of people (for example big secular congregations at important festivals)? Or could it be that size was an expression of wealth, an expression of honour both to God and the saint whose house the church was? Height and length lent solemnity to ritual, especially processions, and allowed spatial, almost theatrical, effects in the liturgy. Size also allowed space for numerous subsidiary altars, representing a company of saints.

Saints and cults

The cult of saints permeated medieval religion and society. Saints were holy men and women who were believed to radiate special power. The Latin word for this power was *virtus*, meaning something like 'force' or 'potency'. Saints continued to radiate *virtus* after they died, which is why their graves and remains became centres of devotion and religious tourism - pilgrimage.

Anything which came into contact or close proximity with a saint was itself charged with *virtus*. Hence, the temporary resting places of saints and items of clothing or objects which touched them were also deeply venerated or highly sought after.

Saints were believed to be close to God, and could thus act as intermediaries between heaven and earth. Kings and aristocrats who endowed great churches might look to their patrons saints for support in temporal affairs. Interest in saints helps to explain the considerable number of side altars and chapels which existed both in great and parish churches. Each altar invoked its own saint, and many contained relics.

ABOVE: St Alban's Cathedral, showing the great length of the nave.

LEFT: Old Sarum, Wiltshire: a Norman cathedral complex within a former Iron Age hillfort. Early in the thirteenth century the cathedral was abandoned in favour of a new site nearby: Salisbury.

LEFT: Altar-shrine, Whitchurch Canicorum, Dorset. The niches enabled those who venerated the saint to place themselves in close proximity to the relic(s).

BELOW: York Minster, a view from the west. The visible cathedral building is mostly Gothic, with architectural styles from c1230 to c1472. On the right of the Minster is one of 19 surviving parish churches in York (there were 45 by 1300). It is St Michael-le-Belfrey, probably earlier than thirteenth century but rebuilt completely in 1525-37.

Council for British Archaeology

Anonymous individual, possibly an architect, in the chapter house at Southwell, Nottinghamshire. This may be a self-portrait.

Masons and architects

Absorbing questions with which pupils can engage directly arise from the construction of great churches. How were they designed, and how were designs realised?

Lessons in the use of sources can be learned from how earlier historians approached these questions. Some Victorian scholars imagined that great churches were built by monks, or that medieval people were gifted with a facility for cooperative action which society has since lost.

One reason why some early scholars held fallacious ideas about design and building was their lack of accessible sources and experience in using them. Surviving medieval building accounts had not been fully studied or published. The fact that such records tended to be kept by monks or clerics (by definition, the people most likely to be literate and numerate: 'clerk') created an impression that building projects were entirely run by monks.

This supposition was reinforced by the dearth of original design drawings. In retrospect, this should not have been surprising. Working documents become expendable when the work is finished. In an age before photocopiers it would be surprising if many project drawings of the medieval period had come down to us. (Could you find the working drawings for your school

or your house?) However, until the sixteenth century designers worked more on vellum than on paper. Vellum was valuable, and often re-used so that earlier designs were erased. Here is a good illustration of the historian's maxim that absence of evidence is not always evidence of absence!

Even so, a few examples of project drawings have survived in different parts of Europe. They demonstrate that project drawings were used, and that the people behind them had strong creative personalities. Models were also used, sometimes for demonstration purposes, to show a patron what (s)he was getting.

The author of such designs (no female medieval architects have yet been recognised) was called *magister*, 'master', or *magister operi*, 'master of the works'. Usually they were masons, but some were master carpenters. The role they fulfilled was wider and more 'hands on' than that of a modern architect, often embracing the work of the contractor, engineer, and site manager, as well as designer. Some medieval masters are known to us by name. Occasionally we meet their faces, usually in sculpture or on a tomb, staring out across the centuries from the buildings they designed.

Medieval buildings: Making the drawings

Medieval builders worked without optical instruments like the level (which measures relative height) or theodolite (which measures angles). Nor did they use standardised measures, although there is evidence for unusual different units of measure at different times and places, an measuring rods. How, then, did they prepare a site and set out a design at full scale?

Geometry is the key. Sophisticated layouts can be scaled up or down, and transferred from design to site, without mathematical calculation.

The stone grave cover of a master mason of the fifteenth century from Crowland Abbey, Lincolnshire. The inscription reads, 'Here lies Master William of Wermington, the Mason, on the soul of whom God of His Grace gave absolution'. His effigy holds a proportional set square and compasses and is shown wearing a monk's cowl and a long flowing robe.

Crowland Abbey

MEDIEVAL CHAPELS

The word chapel as we use it today covers two broad and distinctly different kinds of building:

■ a church (or part of a church) which was secondary to a main church

■ a place of worship for nonconformists.

Historically, a chapel was a church of secondary or satellite status. The word seems to derive from Latin *capella* a 'cloak' (the underlying sense may have been 'shelter'). Medieval chapels ranged from small, simple buildings to large and elaborate churches which were founded after the parishes were defined, usually during or after the twelfth century.

Parochial chapels often served people who lived in outlying parts of the parish, or found it difficult for people to reach the parish church at certain times of year (for example, because of long distances, swollen rivers or impassable roads): hence, 'chapel-of-ease'.

Such chapels were institutionally subordinate to the mother church of the parish (see page 3 for a modern example). For the same reason, 'chapel' can also refer to a subsidiary part of a parish church or cathedral, with its own altar.

Chapels

No one knows how many chapels existed in medieval England, but it is clear that there were many thousands of them, of different kinds. For example:

■ mortuary or charnel chapel: associated with a cemetery or for storing bones

■ manorial chapel: a room for family worship attached to a manor house or other magnate residence

■ well chapel: upon or beside a spring (from the Old English word *wylla*, 'spring') or pool, often credited with miraculous properties of healing or augury

■ gate, bridge or causeway chapels: for the convenience of travellers who could pray for safe passage as they set out on journeys (which were often risky) or give thanks upon return

■ chantry chapel: either within a church or a building in its own right, where masses were said or sung for the soul of the founder.

Most chapels were abandoned after the Reformation and have disappeared. Their sites are often lost and await discovery. Sources likely to give clues to a chapel's former existence include:

■ Chantry certificates. A chantry was an endowment for a priest or chapel or altar.

■ Maps (usually located in the county record office)

ABOVE: Odda's Chapel, Deerhurst, Glos. Founded c 1055, the close relationship between this chapel and the neighbouring (later) house reminds us of the close connection which existed between church founding and local landowners.

BELOW: Gate church of St Swithun, Winchester. Medieval long-distance travel was difficult and sometimes dangerous. Town gates were points at which to say a prayer or make an offering to safeguard a forthcoming journey, or give thanks for one completed.

■ Field and place names: where such sources have been examined, the whereabouts of chapels which have vanished may be noted in Sites and Monuments Records (see page 36)

■ Antiquarian drawings

■ Archaeological air photographs.

Mick Sharp

Council for British Archaeology

NONCONFORMIST BUILDINGS

Since the sixteenth century the word chapel has acquired another meaning. From around the time of the Civil War it also came to denote buildings used by nonconformists or dissenters - so called because they dissented from some of the doctrines of the Church of England and wished to meet or worship separately. Hence, while Anglicans go to church, Methodists or Baptists go to chapel.

Some nonconformist denominations, like the Quakers, do not engage in organised worship at all. Their buildings are called meeting houses.

Meeting houses

Broadly speaking, the Civil War can be taken as the starting point for an independent tradition of nonconformist building.

Dissenters of many different kinds - for example Baptists (General and Particular), Quakers, Independents, Congregationalists - existed sooner, but it was after the 1640s, and particularly after the Toleration Act 1689, that nonconformists began to erect buildings of their own.

Nonconformity and buildings

Nonconformity, almost by definition, involves diversity of opinion, reflected in a correspondingly wide range of building types. Leading (but not universal) themes in the arrangements of chapels include provision for prayer, sermons and hymns. Hence, furnishings, fittings and galleries often contribute much to a chapel's historical interest.

The smallest, more remote chapels and meeting houses are sometimes characterised by a strong vernacular feel, using materials, proportions and features which may also appear in other local buildings. As nonconformity gained in strength and social respectability, so larger and more elaborate chapels were constructed, on more prominent sites. The progression from modest buildings in the hinterlands of domestic property to conspicuous high street locations is one which can be followed in many market towns and cities.

RIGHT: Methodist Church built in 1899 as the Primitive Methodist Meeting Hall, Kendal, Cumbria.

TOP LEFT: **Puritan chapel of mid-seventeenth century, built by Sir Robert Dyneley in the grounds of his house at Bramhope, West Yorkshire.**
TOP RIGHT: **Quaker meeting house and cemetery in Bury St. Edmunds, Suffolk.**
ABOVE LEFT: **One of five preaching stations established in 1843-5 by Lion Walk Congregational Church, Colchester at Old Heath, known locally as the 'Tin Tabernacle'.**
ABOVE RIGHT: **Baptist Church at Thorpe, in Essex, built in 1802.**

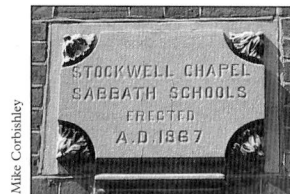

ABOVE: **Plaque to Stockwell St chapel.**

ABOVE: **Stockwell Street chapel, Colchester Essex.**
RIGHT: **United Reformed Church in Kendal, Cumbria.**
BELOW RIGHT: **Standing at the side of an alley in Tewkesbury, Gloucestershire, The Old Baptist Chapel was formed in the seventeenth century from an existing timber-framed hall-house of c.1500.**

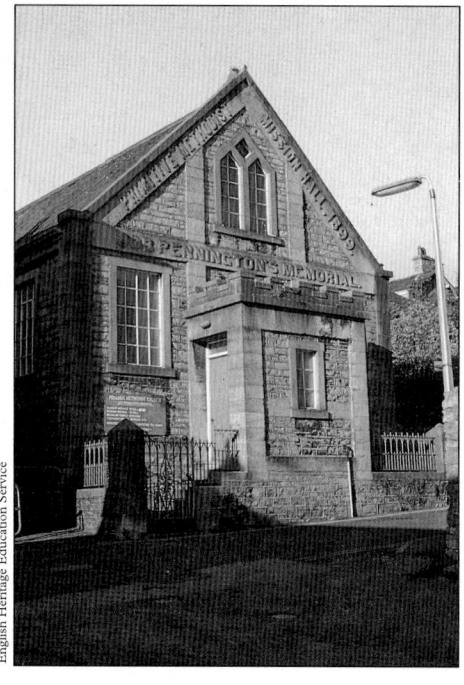

Architectural styles

Chapel-builders in the nineteenth century took little direct part in the battle of the styles which gripped the Church of England. However, they did find ways of proclaiming their institutional distinctiveness. Classical forms, for instance, largely abandoned by Anglicans after the 1840s, remained popular with many nonconformists for some time afterwards. The tower, another feature reminiscent of Anglicanism and its medieval past, was at first commonly avoided.

As time passed the significance of stylistic symbolism waned. Many nonconformist buildings have been built in an idiom of medieval or Gothic revival pastiche, and towards the end of the nineteenth century a number were designed to rival the Anglicans in architectural splendour. In Halifax, for instance, Church of England and Congregationalist mill-owners built grand churches in different parts of the town. From a distance, so high do their steeples soar, a new visitor might find it difficult to guess where their denominational allegiances lay.

Change in chapel buildings

Unlike most parish churches, chapels and meeting houses may at first glance sometimes seems like architectural 'single statements' - that is, that they were built in one campaign. However, closer study will commonly reveal alterations and different phases of work, and the same archaeological principles of study as apply to parish churches are relevant for nonconformist chapels.

Bear in mind that as these buildings were begun much later than most parish churches, it is often possible to date them from written records as well as by study of their fabrics. Many chapels display foundation- or date-stones: evidence which is both documentary and archaeological. But be careful: such stones were sometimes re-used and so may not date the wall they are in.

BELOW: The Baptist chapel at Goodshaw, Lancashire, now in the care of English Heritage, is one of very few which has been the subject of archaeological excavation.

INSET: The interior of the chapel shows eighteenth-century box pews with numbered doors and a gallery on three sides.

GOODSHAW CHAPEL

WHAT WENT ON IN A CHURCH?

Each part of a church had a particular use or uses, some of which changed as time passed. These included:

The nave (from Latin *navis*, 'a ship', a common symbol for the Church) was the place of ordinary people. Here parishioners stood or sat (little is known about seating before the late fourteenth century, when benches began to be introduced) to listen to and watch the mass. Benches were sometimes incorporated into the walls of the nave. The origin of the phrase 'the sick go to the wall' comes from this feature. Sermons became increasingly important after about 1300, and some churches contain a medieval pulpit.

Other features in the nave would be a font, in which people would be initiated to the Church, and one or more subsidiary altars (see below, p.15). Nave walls would often be limewashed and painted with episodes of religious devotion - some of a quasi-mythological character - and sometimes a representation of Purgatory or the Last Judgement.

The chancel (which literally means an enclosure) was the eastern part of the church. It contained the principal altar, and was screened off and set apart for use by the officiating clergy.

Aisles Flanking the nave, and sometimes the chancel, were often one or more aisles (from Latin *ala*, 'a wing'). Today these look like overflow space for the congregation, but in the medieval period aisles were often compartmentalised, the different portions being set apart as family burial chapels, and for the use of guilds.

Entrance Parishioners usually entered the church by a nave door sometimes sheltered by a porch. This was a special place - the boundary between the secular world and the realm of the spirit - and the point at which important ceremonies (like burial, baptism and marriage) began. Because of their special, frontier, status porches were also places for sealing bargains, making vows, and confirming business transactions.

Furnishings and fittings will help pupils to reconstruct how churches were used at different times.

Medieval use focused on altars, and related objects of devotion like statues of saints, or the rood (an Old English word for cross) which often stood on a screen that divided the chancel from the nave. Virtually all churches - even very small ones - contained at least two or three altars; some had more.

English Heritage Photo Library

ABOVE: St Swithun's Church, Compton Beauchamp, Oxfordshire, thirteenth-century wall paintings.

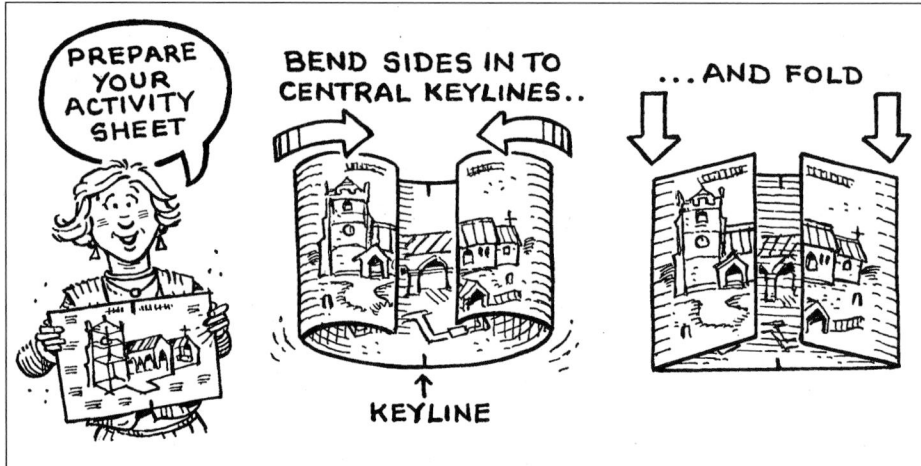

The photocopiable family activities on the next two pages of this book were originally drawn and designed as part of the *History at Home* project in Cumbria. You may photocopy them and fold them using the key lines.

DETAILS AND CLUES TO LOOK FOR THE PARISH

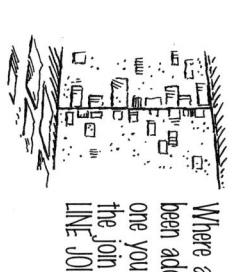

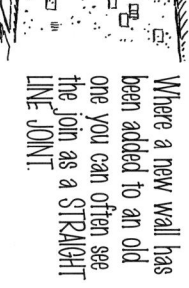

What do you think it is made from? Brick or stone? Or something else?

What shape are the windows? Are there any clues which show that the church was built at different times? You could look for blocked-up windows and doors, different styles of windows, different types and age of building material, straight line joints.

Is the church on a hill, or is it in the middle of lots of shops or houses? Does it stand out from the buildings around it?

The lychgate marks the entrance to the churchyard.

WINDOW STYLES
The shape of church windows changed over centuries, and gives a good indication of date.

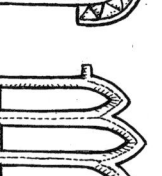

Norman c.1100AD

Early English c 1200AD

Decorated c.1300AD

Perpendicular c.1400AD

Where a new wall has been added to an old one you can often see the join as a STRAIGHT LINE JOINT.

ROOD SCREEN separated the clergy in the chancel from the congregation in the nave. Rood means the Cross.

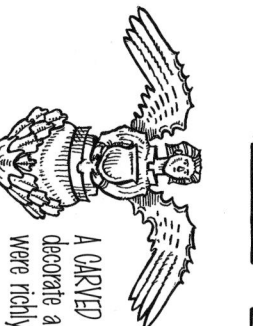

A CARVED ANGEL used to decorate a roof. They were richly coloured.

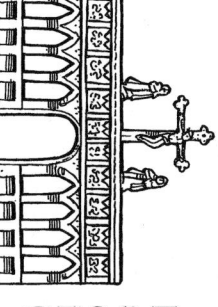

A PILLAR is a column which has at its top a CAPITAL, which is often carved.

TRIPLE DECKER PULPIT
The parish clerk sat in the lower deck, while the parson read the service from the middle deck, but preached from the top deck.

BOX PEWS
were originally paid for by the richer members of the parish. In the eighteenth century they became popular for all members of the congregation. They helped keep out the draughts.

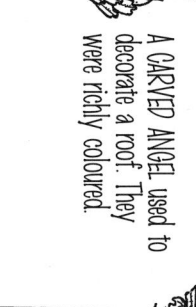

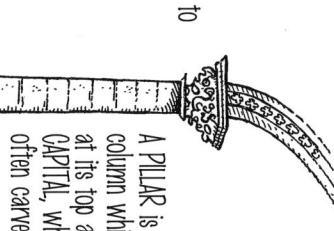

This activity was devised as part of the History at Home project. It has been re-drawn by Dai Owen. c English Heritage 1996.

Is there a church near you? Does it look new or old? Is it tall with a high tower like this one or does it have a spire?

Does it have a clock like this one?

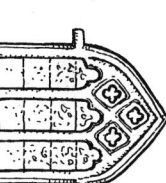

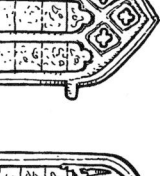

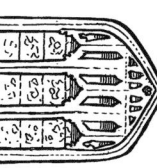

Does it have a churchyard with gravestones? Are these all the same shape or not? What is the oldest date you can find on a gravestone? Do the styles of gravestones change?

Yew trees have often grown in graveyards for centuries.

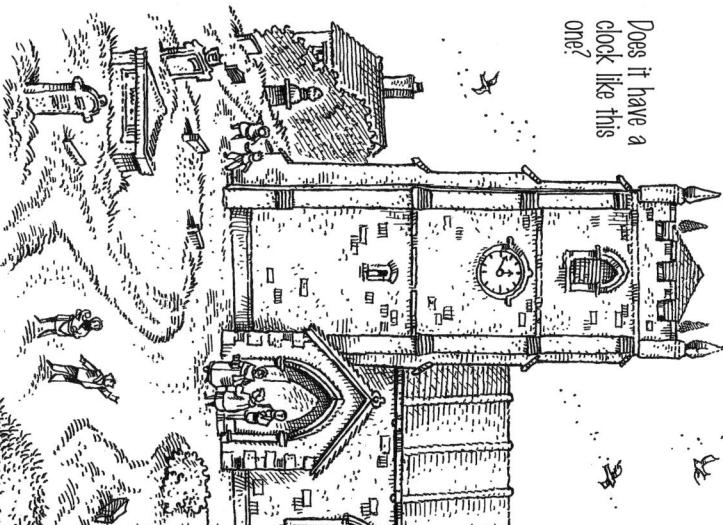

THINGS TO LOOK FOR INSIDE

A church is used for Christian worship. Do you see this symbol anywhere?

As you walk inside a church, what do you notice first? Is it very quiet and still, or are there lots of people around, the sound of traffic outside?

MEMORIALS
There may be some writing on walls of the church. What is it about? Are there different kinds of memorials? Do you recognize any of the local names? Sometimes important people were buried inside the church in carved tombs.

THE BELLS
The bells are rung to summon people to services. Can you see where they are hung? How are they rung?

PARISH CHEST
Is there an old wooden chest in the church? This is the Parish Chest in which documents used to be kept. It usually had three locks. The vicar and churchwardens each kept a key and they all had to be present to open the chest. Why do you think there were three keys?

THE ARCHES
Have a look at the arches. Round headed arches are usually older than pointed ones. What shapes are the capitals plain or decorated?

MUSIC
When people sing in this church, do they have an organ or a piano to help them?

THE PULPIT
What is it made from? Sometimes triple decker pulpits survive.

THE ROOF
In very big churches you may find a stone vault, but most churches have a wooden roof. Some old roofs are beautifully decorated with angels and coats of arms.

CHANCEL

NAVE

CHRISTENING
Is there a font for children to be christened?

SEATS
Where are people meant to sit? Are there wooden pews, or individual chairs? The seats are usually in the NAVE. Some churches still have very old pews with doors, known as box pews.

GLASS
Are the windows full of clear glass or stained glass? Can you tell whether the stained glass is very modern or Victorian? Occasionally some medieval glass survives.

THE ALTAR
All the seats in church face the same way. As you sit down you will be facing a table, altar, or holy table. Can you find out what it is used for? If it's covered does it have a special colour? What is on it? The altar is up a step in the CHANCEL in the wall by the altar you will sometimes see a recess for the holy water stoop and a small cupboard called an aumbrey.

When people read the Bible in church, is there a special place to read it from? There might be an eagle carved into the stand or lectern. The eagle is a symbol of the resurrection and ascension of Jesus.

Council for British Archaeology

Squints either side of the chancel arch in the small, aiseless church at Ashley, Hampshire, suggest that the church contained at least two altars at the east end of the nave.

Extra altars allowed dedications to additional saints (see page 12), and could be a focus for the identity of groupings within the parish, such as a prominent family, a group of neighbours who belonged to a fraternity (a kind of club which combined social and religious activity), or a guild.

Clues to former altar positions include squints (holes bored through masonry to allow sight-lines between different altars), corbels or image housings for statues of saints, aumbries and piscinas (cupboards and washing places for the Eucharistic vessels). Subsidiary altar positions may also point to the former whereabouts of chantries.

AFTER THE REFORMATION

After the Reformation people were instructed to believe that statues, images and saints were idolatrous. Statues and altar slabs were thrown out, or in some cases hidden in the hope that a time would come when they could be reinstated. Wallpaintings were whitewashed over. This is why, even today, medieval wall paintings are sometimes hidden behind limewash and await rediscovery.

Parish worship between the Civil War and the early years of Victoria's reign was mainly about sitting, listening and singing. Altars were reduced to one - now a wooden table - and emphasis in worship shifted from the mass to prayer-book liturgy and sermons, reflected still in some churches where a pulpit incorporating a clerks' desk still survives.

New-built churches

New churches of this period commonly consisted of a rectangular nave with galleries, designed to bring everyone within easy hearing distance of the pulpit. Since the importance of the Eucharist was downplayed (such a service might only be held once a year) the chancel was unimportant, often consisting of no more than a shallow recess.

But there was continuity too. The medieval tradition of the parish church tower, and bells, remained strong. So too did the influence of local lords. The squire's pew, high-sided, often prominently placed, sometimes with its own fireplace and private door, reminds us of eighteenth-century Sundays when sermons were long and the Anglican squirearchy still looked upon the local church as 'theirs'.

Council for British Archaeology

Fourteenth-century altar, reset, in the parish church at Asthall, Oxfordshire.

RIGHT: Carved pew ends from the Church of St Andrew, Aysgarth, North Yorkshire.

English Heritage Photo Library

WHEN WERE CHURCHES BUILT?

Whatever they look like today, bear in mind that most of England's parish churches originated in just two epochs: the years of later Anglo-Saxon and early Norman England (roughly, AD 900-1150), and the nineteenth century. In between, parish churches were often modernised or rebuilt, but less often founded.

The table, on this page, gives a rough idea of the sequence of events.

THE FOUNDING OF LOCAL CHURCHES: 950-1150

Churchfounding was at its height between the late nineth and twelfth centuries. The Church itself had little hand in it. The work seems to have been undertaken mainly by local lords, sometimes their wives or widows, who built churches for themselves, families and households on their estates, and treated them as private property. Only rather later were these buildings broadened into public use, coming to be regarded as in some sense everybody's concern and under the control of the bishop rather than a lay order.

Local landholders may have been keen to have churches of their own as special burial places, in imitation of the royalty and aristocracy who founded and endowed monasteries, to ensure a steady stream of prayers for their souls after they died.

Clues to this proprietary context for many churches are often visible today. The link between churches and centres of local secular power is often witnessed in the juxtaposition of a church and a manor house or motte-and-bailey castle.

The growing network of churches in private hands created a challenge to the authority of the Church. To whom, for instance, was a local priest answerable: the lord who appointed him, or his bishop?

In the twelfth century bishops tackled this problem by extending their authority over local churches.

Royal Commission on the Historical Monuments of England

The intimate relationship between church and motte-and-bailey at Burton-in-Lonsdale, North Yorkshire, reminds us that the site was closely controlled by a Norman lord in the twelfth century.

900-1150: most medieval parish churches founded

1100-1200: rebuilding on a larger scale almost always now in stone

1200-1500: piecemeal enlargement

1540-1650: destruction of medieval patterns of worship

1650-1800: prayerbooks and preachers

1800-1900: industrial revolution and Gothic revival: many new parish churches built, especially in expanding industrial towns

Cathedrals

Foundation		First main building date witnessed by surviving fabric
600	Canterbury	1070
604	London	?1675-1710 (Wren)
642	Winchester	late 11th century
655-870	Peterborough	early 12th century
673	Ely	late 11th century
676	Hereford	early 12th century
680	Worcester	1084
681	Gloucester	1089
c690	Exeter	early 12th century
704	Wells	late 12th century
727	Oxford	1150
793	St Albans	late 11th century
954	Lincoln	1092
997	Durham	1093
1075	Chichester	late 11th century
1076	Old Sarum	late 11th century
1077	Rochester	1077-80
1080	York	1080-1100
1092	Carlisle	late 11th century
1094	Norwich (moved to Norwich)	
1227	Salisbury (transferred from Old Sarum)	

Later on, churches are sometimes found next to great houses, or marooned in parks following the clearance of the settlements that accompanied them. Such settings, though hundreds of years later than the dates of origin, may nevertheless point back to the period when churches belonged to local magnates.

RIGHT: The medieval church at Sledmere, N Yorkshire, has been engulfed in a landscaped park surrounding the great house.

Development and rebuilding

This illustration shows the growth of a parish church from small and simple beginnings in the tenth or eleventh century to a large, developed plan by the end of the medieval period. Darkly shaded areas represent floor space available for general congregational use.

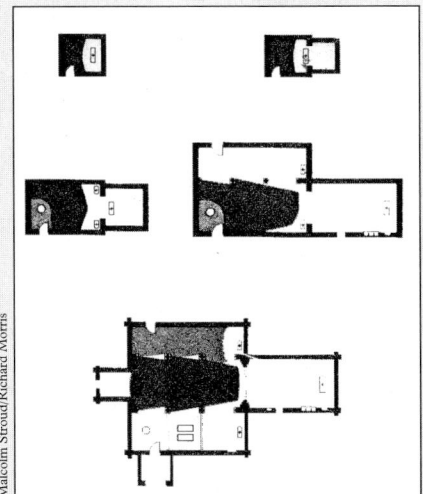

The expansion in size is not wholly explained by the need to accommodate more people: a desire on the part of important families and fraternities or guilds to treat parts of the church as 'theirs' (for example for family tombs, or special altars dedicated to favoured saints) is also involved. The floor area reaches its largest extent after the great famines and epidemics of the fourteenth century, when England's population may have been halved.

Only a minority of churches was ever comprehensively rebuilt. More usually, modernisation took place by a series of additions made at different times. A common way of modernising a church was to cut new, more fashionable, windows through existing walls. Similarly, small churches of the eleventh and twelfth centuries were often enlarged by the addition of aisles and side chapels, with arcades pierced through the original structure. Signs of these processes are commonly visible.

Other clues to an origin that may be a good deal older than today's structure can include:

■ Anglo-Saxon or Viking-age carved stones, either re-used in the fabric or loose in the church. Such stones are usually gravestones, and may indicate the former presence of an associated church which is earlier than the present building.

■ Older architectural fragments which have been re-used. Try to ascertain how such pieces would have been used originally: what do they tell us about the appearance of the earlier church?

■ Features like doors or windows which have been pierced through older walls.

A few churches were never much changed, and remain close to their original size and layout in the eleventh or twelfth century.

Some churches, like this twelfth-century building at Up Waltham, Sussex, have changed little since they were built. Even here, however, notice that there have been changes in window style and position. The presence of earlier windows is ghosted in the rendering.

REBUILDING AND ENLARGEMENT: 1100-1300

Churches founded before the end of the Anglo-Saxon period (roughly, by 1050) are thought mainly to have been built of wood. Placenames like 'Woodchurch' or 'Woodkirk' remind us of this, and archaeological fieldwork is beginning to confirm it.

Wood decays fairly rapidly, so Anglo-Saxon timber churches had limited lives. (Only one example, at Greenstead, Essex, recently dated to the second half of the eleventh century, is known to have survived.) In any case, from the early eleventh century the fashion grew of replacing timber churches with larger buildings constructed of stone. Many hundreds of eleventh/early twelfth-century buildings remain in use, while in thousands of other cases these generally simple, two- or three-cell plans became the nuclei for later enlargement.

INDUSTRIAL REVOLUTION AND GOTHIC REVIVAL: 1800-1900

The second great age of church founding corresponded with urban growth and rising population of the Industrial Revolution. Hence, many churches were built in expanding towns. Unlike their medieval predecessors, most can be exactly dated. Often we know who built them, and in some cases correspondence and drawings for the new buildings survive in archives.

Positions of churches can tell us much about the stages of urban economic development: for example where workers lived, the catchment areas of particular businesses; or the siting of a church for aesthetic reasons as part of calculated town planning.

Styles reflect links between architecture and theological theory. Some nineteenth-century churchmen regarded Gothic as a uniquely Christian style.

Council for British Archaeology

Like hundreds of other churches, St Botolph, Bossall, N Yorkshire was rebuilt in the twelfth century, on a larger scale than its predecessor. While many parish churches of this period were built on an axial plan - that is, with tower, nave and chancel in line - St Botolphs has a cruciform layout, like a miniature version of a cathedral.

✠ CHVRCH·OF·THE·HOLY·TRINITY·VPPER·CHELSEA: NOW IN COVRSE OF ERECTION·J·D·SEDDING·ARCHT

Ground Plan.

J D Sedding Archt

Royal Commission on the Historical Monuments of England

RIGHT: Drawing Holy Trinity, Sloane Street, Chelsea, London by J D Shelding. The church, built in 1888-90 is largely Arts and Craft Gothic in style.

Preferences for particular denominations sometimes show us the allegiances of patrons (for example millowners, machine manufacturers). In time, certain towns became dominated by families with religious emphases to match.

Diversity - or the lack of it - may echo the economic structure of a town. Britain's industrial cities in the nineteenth century were not uniform. Manchester, for instance, was in the hands of relatively few textile masters, whereas Birmingham flourished through specialisation in metalworking trades, reflected in greater religious diversity.

While fashionable resorts of high society like Tunbridge Wells, Bath, Cheltenham or Brighton had central churches for the upper classes, such places also had their working-class areas, with churches and chapels to serve them.

Anglo-Catholic attitudes

During the nineteenth century 'prayerbook' interiors were usually cleared out. Many Victorians wished to reinstate Eucharistic worship. The importance of the chancel was thus restored, and there were widespread efforts to return church interiors to what was imagined as a more medieval, 'catholic' format.

Commonly, it is the Victorian interior with its stone pulpit, pews, painted woodwork and choir stalls which is still in use today. Learned textbooks were produced which prescribed the appearance and layout of furnishings, fittings, and different floor levels. These layouts were more fantasy than facsimile: in many respects, Victorian clergy and architects had no idea what medieval church interiors had actually looked like.

ABOVE: St Bartholemew's church, Ann Street, Brighton, designed by E E Scott and built in 1872-74.

BELOW: Interior of the church of St George, Stockport, Cheshire built in 1893-97.

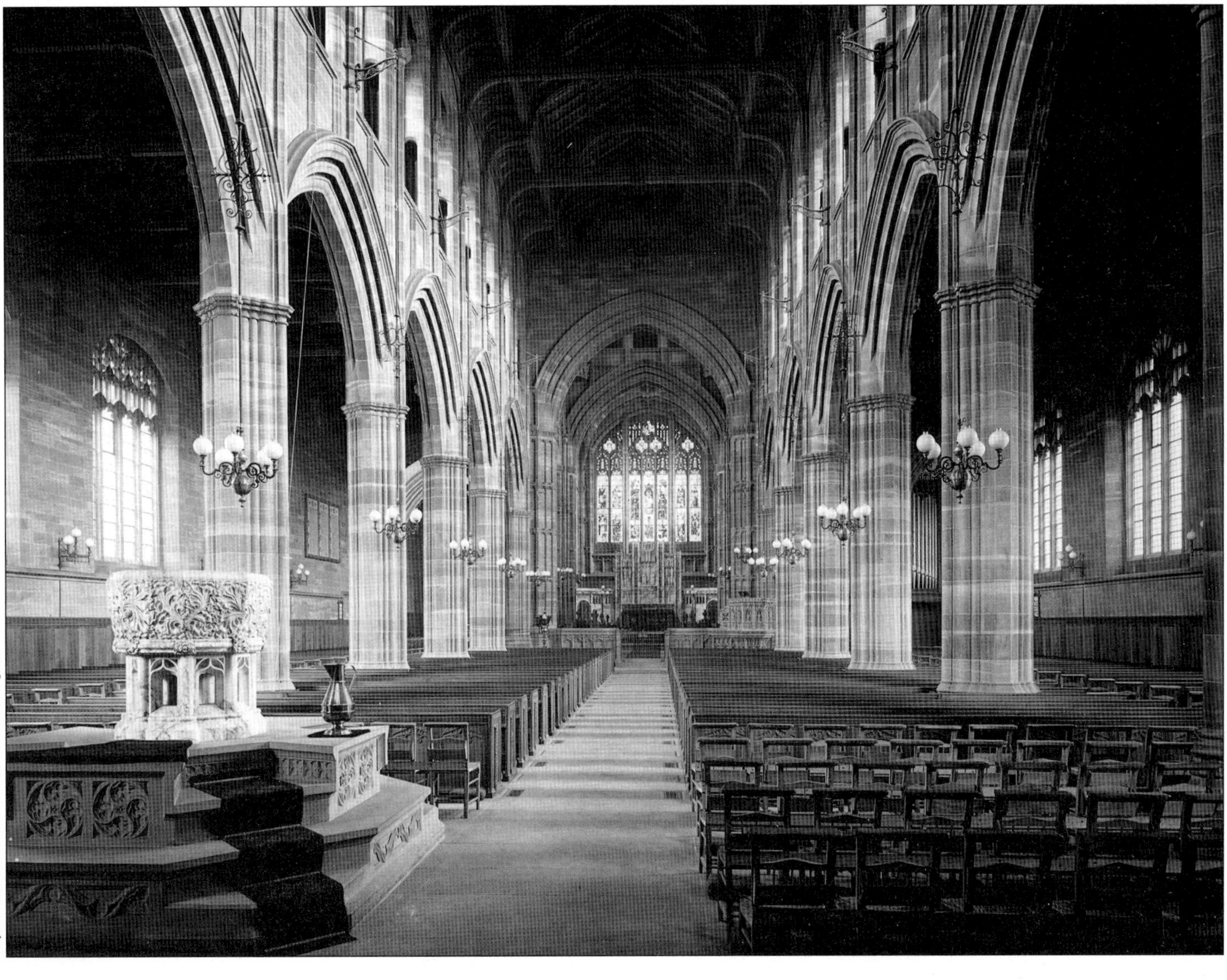

UNDER AND AROUND THE CHURCH

BELOW THE FLOOR

Inside a church you could ask you pupils to work out what might lie below the floor. Useful clues include:

■ Inscribed grave slabs, suggesting burials beneath (but are such slabs in their original positions?)

Graveslab decorated with a shroud in the pavement of a church at Norbury, Derbyshire.

■ Slabs with iron rings or hand-holds (intended for periodic lifting, giving access to family vaults or brick-lined shafts)

■ Remains to do with the development of the building. For instance, if an arcade has been cut through an earlier wall, the columns may be standing on the foundations or reduced wall of the previous building (see Avebury church page 31).

Buried remains which may not be signposted in the floor or fabric, but may nevertheless be present, could include:

■ Traces of an earlier church (for example of Anglo-Saxon or early Norman date)

■ Archaeological evidence for use of the site before the church was founded (for example traces of prehistoric or Roman agriculture or occupation).

RIGHT: Rudston, East Yorkshire: prehistoric monolith (in an area rich in prehistoric sites) beside the parish church.

Visible within the church may be features which help us to reconstruct former rituals. Common examples include:

■ Squints, which help locate sites of former altars

■ Rood stairs, pointing to the site of a vanished chancel screen. Rood stairs themselves are often blocked up but some traces may remain.

■ Slots (that is, 'chases') representing fixings of former timber screen work, dividing up side chapels, or post-Reformation furnishings (like box pews, often stripped out by the Victorians).

St. Mary's Church, Little Oakley, Essex. Excavations inside the church revealed the burial of a priest of the late twelfth century.

Rood stair in Great Oakley parish church, Essex.

Excavating a church

Nave of parish church of St Edmund, Kellington, North Yorkshire, under excavation in late December 1990 in advance of engineering works to prevent mining subsidence. The camera looks east, towards the chancel. The ragged pits towards the right of the picture are shafts of seventeenth and eighteenth-century graves which have been excavated by archaeologists. The earthen channel which runs up the centre of the photo marks the central aisle, wherein many graves were dug between the box pews that existed to left and right in the eighteenth century. The south wall of the nave (to right) dates from the late eleventh century. The arcade of the north aisle stands upon the reduced wall of its northern counterpart. At the top of the picture can be seen the bases of walls which projected inwards to frame a narrow Norman chancel arch, below a much wider arch that was inserted in the nineteenth century. Cobble foundations in the foreground carried the eleventh-century west wall. Patches of white stone within the nave originally formed a complete rectangle which was subsequently dissected by grave-digging and other disturbances. The rectangle was probably the foundation for a small late-Anglo-Saxon church. Remains under the floor of your local church may be no less complicated than these.

20

OUT IN THE CHURCHYARD

If your church is of medieval origin it is likely that the churchyard will contain burials going back for up to a thousand years. Some churchyards are older still. The churchyard may either be larger or of different shape to the first cemetery, and careful study of its surface and boundaries may give clues to such changes of outline.

Churchyard monuments

Medieval churchyard monuments rarely survive in their original positions, but they are commonly found re-used as building material in the church, or in churchyard walls.

Medieval gravestones re-used as coping stones on the churchyard wall at Skipwith, Humberside.

Features and structures which are sometimes to be seen in churchyards include:

Lychgate Entrance structure to the churchyard, taking its name from the Anglo-Saxon word for corpse: *lic* (pronounced 'lich').

Churchyard cross An important feature in medieval processional ritual. Commonly, only the cross bases survive.

RIGHT: Churchyard cross base at Raunds, Northamptonshire.

Bell-cage

Bells were sometimes hung in a free-standing structure of wood or stone. Medieval records disclose that bells could also be hung from trees.

Schoolhouse The teaching of pupils was sometimes a supplementary duty of chaplains or chantry priests (priest paid to say masses for the souls of the dead). Chantry duties were not unduly onerous and left time available for the education of local children. In the fifteenth and sixteenth centuries literacy was becoming more widespread. After the Reformation, money and bequests which had previously been channelled into chantries (masses for the souls of the dead) was sometimes redirected towards alternative charitable provision, like schools.

Dwellings Medieval or sixteenth/seventeenth-century houses sometimes stand on the fringe of the churchyard. In certain cases these were built by the rector or parish to provide rental income.

Charnel house A building to contain human bones which were either periodically gathered when burial became too dense, or else collected when they were disturbed. Some charnel houses were underground chambers (for example below the floor of the porch)

Bell-cage, probably from the seventeenth century at Wrabness, Essex.

ABOVE: Bones gathered in the charnel house at Hythe, Kent.

Mausoleum A structure, usually of the seventeenth to nineteenth centuries, for the dead of a local family of high status.

Of course, there are gravestones of parishioners who have died within the last two or three centuries. These may only be the most recent monuments, which are likely to have displaced earlier memorials as a result of continuous burial on consecrated ground.

ABOVE: Eighteenth-century family mausoleum in the churchyard of All Saints, Little Ouseburn, N Yorkshire.

Archaeology and churches

Archaeologists investigate the evidence for religion in a variety of ways, by:

■ locating evidence from maps, other documents or from aerial photographs

The group of buildings showing here a mark in the crop are probably Nowers Manor in Norfolk. The church (on the left with an apse at the east end) is most likely the chapel of St Nicholas mentioned in records in 1310 and 1430. It was probably once the parish church but became a chapel to the manor in the fifteenth century. The large building to the south is probably the manorial hall.

■ excavating inside or around the church building

■ investigating and recording the fabric of the building itself.

At St Andrew's Church, Wroxeter in Shropshire careful work by archaeologists from the University of Birmingham has revealed details about the building's history (see also page 31).

From this archaeological work it has been possible suggest a sequence of buildings and artist's impressions of each main period.

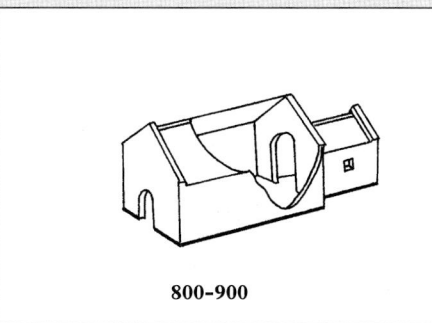

800-900

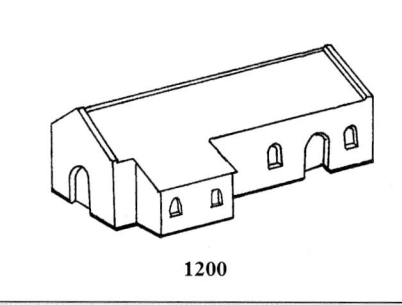

1200

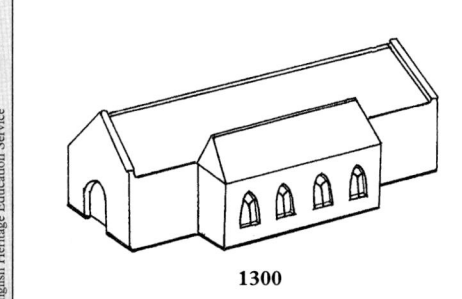

1300

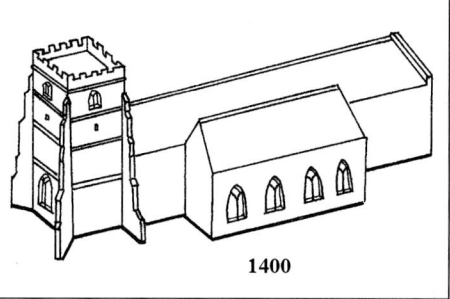

1400

Wroxeter, Shropshire. An artist's impressions of the main phases of building.

LEFT: Wroxeter church (see also pages 23 and 31), Shropshire.

Wroxeter, Shropshire. Stone-by-stone drawing of the north side of the church.

REPAIR, RESTORATION AND RE-USE

Victorian parish churches often illustrate the distinction between restoration and repair - concepts which play a large part in conservation philosophy today:

■ Restoration is an attempt to restore a building to its supposed appearance at some former stage in its history.

■ Restoration requires the 'cleansing' of extraneous features which are older or younger than the stylistic stage to which the building is returned.

■ Repair is simply the renewal of worn-out fabric. This approach respects all parts of a church for what they are. Repair can be tactful and non-assertive, and where new work is needed for structural reasons, it may be differentiated from what was there before - a new contribution rather than an attempt to replicate.

■ Repair can also include 'conservation' techniques, where the original material is preserved in its current state, but not renewed or copied.

Nineteenth-century restorers destroyed much Norman and late-medieval church fabric, and seventeenth/eighteenth-century furnishings, in their efforts to reinstate the purity of high medieval Gothic. Apart from its destructiveness, an obvious drawback of restoration is the difficulty of deciding precisely to which stage of a building's history it is to be 'returned'.

South Yorkshire Archaeology Service

RIGHT: Repair or restoration? Work to stabilise the church of St Wilfrid, Hickleton, S Yorkshire, fractured by mining subsidence, has resulted in what is effectively a new building.

During the later nineteenth century there was violent antagonism between the restorers and the repairers who wished to cherish churches as they stood. The repairers eventually formed a society: the Society for the Protection of Ancient Buildings. Both the Society and its principles flourish today, although tensions between philosophies of use and conservation are still much in evidence, and pull in different directions:

■ Change to accommodate new patterns of worship

■ Church as it is

■ Repair as facsimile

■ Repair as found

RIGHT: Not all changes to churches occurred long ago. A change in today's styles of worship and the meetings or gatherings associated with church life might result in the addition of an extra room. This sensitively-designed extension to St Andrew's Church, Eaton in Norfolk is by Purcell Miller Tritton and Partners of Norwich.

John Critchley

Maintenance of churches

Over the centuries, constant grave digging in the churchyard has raised the ground surface level, often to an extraordinary amount (see right).

This will usually cause problem of damp seeping into the walls and damaging rendering on the outside or plaster on the inside walls of the church. One remedy often taken by church authorities is to have a channel dug around the church to provide a dry area against the walls. These channels are sometimes filled in with drains and gravel but are more often left open. This work should always be supervised by an archaeologist as valuable evidence may be recorded, for example about earlier phases in the building's history or burials (see far right).

Mike Corbishley

EDUCATIONAL APPROACHES

LOCATION

There are many ways of locating churches and chapels, using maps, other records and discovery in your local environment.

Using documents

From the beginning of the eighteenth century there exist visitation returns for Anglican churches. Questionnaires were sent to each church, to be returned to the bishop. Questions were asked about the provision of education and Sunday schools, the average number who attend divine service, if there were any obstacles to people attending, or whether there are any nonconformist or other places of worship within the parish. Visitation returns will be found in the relevant diocesan record office or in the county record office.

Visitation returns are a good source from which to build up a picture of the state of the Church of England within a parish but other sources are also useful, for example

■ Trades directories

■ Maps and town plans

■ Newspaper reports.

Using the evidence from maps

Churches and chapels are usually marked on maps, at least from the nineteenth century onwards. Early editions of the Ordnance Survey will help you locate a monastery, church or chapel which has disappeared. For some places, estate maps from earlier centuries will contain drawings of churches.

The names of places will often give you a clue, for example:

■ the usual word for a monastery in Old English is *mynster*. It also acquired the derived senses of 'large church' or 'church served by

ABOVE: An extract from the 1865 Visitation Return for Featherstone in Yorkshire.

a community of priests'. The word minster could be added to a person' name, as in Buckminster, Leicestershire (from the name Bucca) or after a physical feature, such as a river, as in Charminster, Dorset, after the River Cerne.

■ the Scandinavian word *kirk*, meaning church, is found in place names in the north and the north Midlands of England. Thus Kirkstead in Lincolnshire means 'site of a church'.

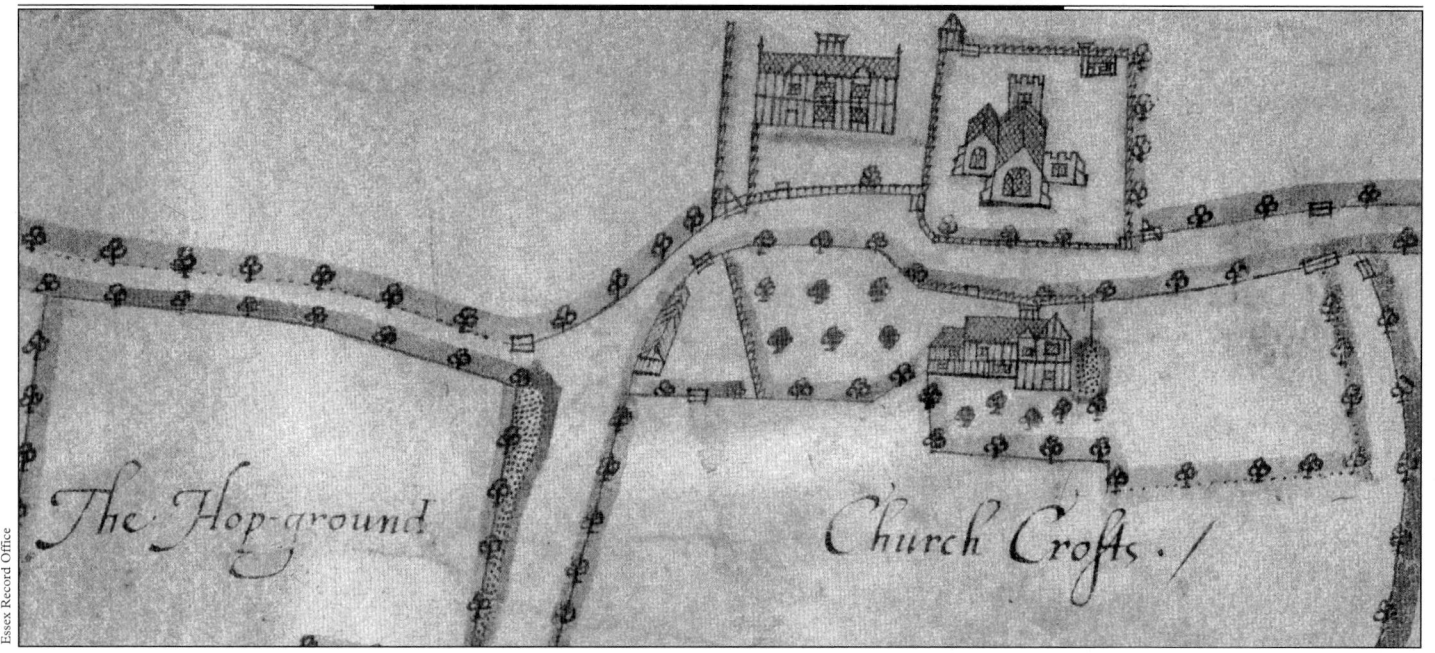

Essex Record Office

The Hop-ground

Church Crofts.

■ fields can be named after churches or chapels, or indicate that the land was owned by the Church. Church Yard in Alveley, Shropshire, Chapel Field in Helion Bumpstead, Essex and Church Way Field ('land on the road to the church') in Holmer, Herefordshire are examples.

Part of estate map of Aldham, Essex of 1639.

Local churches in the Domesday Book

The Domesday survey of 1086 was not primarily concerned with ecclesiastical buildings. Churches, chapels, monasteries and priests are erratically recorded; in some areas a few are mentioned and in others many, but seldom all. In Suffolk, about 360 churches are recorded, while across the border in Essex only 17 are mentioned. It has been estimated that there were between 400 and 450 churches in Suffolk and about 350 in Essex at the time of the survey. The absence of reference to a church is thus an unreliable guide to whether a particular church was in existence by 1086. Archaeological evidence shows, for example, that a church existed at Little Oakley in Essex (see entry below), when the Domesday survey was being carried out.

Plomesgate Hundred, Suffolk. The Count holds Chillesford in lodrship; Ulf, a free man, in the jurisdiction and under the patronage of the Abbot of Ely before 1066; 80 acres as 1 manor. Always 1 villager; 4 smallholders. Then and later 1 ploughs in lordship, now 1; then and later on 1 men's ploughs, now 1. a church, 5 acres of free land. Value 13s 4d. And 3 free men; 20 acres. Always 1 plough. Value 40d.

Public Record Office

> ᚠPLVMESGATA. H̃. Cefefortdaꞌ ten& Comes in dn̅io Olfꞌ
> liƀ hoꞌ In foca & co m̅dat aƀƀis de eli.t.r.e.ꝑ.i.m̅.LXXX.ac.
> fepꞌ.i.uiłł.7.iiii.bor.Tñc 7ꞌꝑ.i.carꞌ 7 dim̅ in dn̅io.m̅.i.Tñc 7
> poftea.i.carꞌ 7 dim̅ hom̅.modo.i.Eccłaꞌ.v.ac̃.liƀæ træꞌ.7 uał
> xiii.foł.7.iiii.đ.Et.iii.liƀi ho̅es.xx.ac̃.fep̃.i.carꞌ.7 uał xL
> denarioS.

Hundred of Tendring, Essex. Germund holds (Little) Oakley from Ralph which Ednoth held as a manor, for 5 hides. Then 7 villagers, now 17. Always 4 smallholders; 8 slaves; 3 ploughs in lordship; 3 men's ploughs. Woodland, 33 pigs; meadow, 2 acres; 1 fishery; pasture, 100 sheep. Then 2 cobs, 13 cattle, 50 pigs, 50 sheep; now 3 cobs, 4 cattle, 27 pigs, 118 sheep. Value then and later £7; now [£]9.

Public Record Office

> ᚠHund de Tendringa. Adem ten&. Germun̅d de.R.qđ tenuit
> Ednod ꝑ Maṅ.7 ꝑ.v.hiđ.7.dim̅.tc̅.vii.uiłł.m̅.xvii.Sep̅.iiii.borđ.
> 7.viii.fer.7.iii.carꞌ.in dn̅io.7.iii.carꞌ.hom̅.Silu̅ꞌxxxiii.porc̃.
> .ii.ac̃.p̃ti.i.pifc̃.Paſt.c.ouꞌtc̅.ii.runc̃.7.xiii.aṅ.L.porc̃.L.ouꞌm̅.
> .iii.runc̃.iiii.aṅ.xxvii.porc̃.cxviii.ouꞌTc̅.7ꞌꝑ uał.vii.liƀ.m̅.ix.

Chapel detectives

Although founded comparatively recently - the majority between the late eighteenth and early twentieth centuries - thousands of nonconformist chapels have disappeared, or have been converted to secular uses. Reasons may include:

■ Overprovision (reflecting times of religious fervour, denominational or congregational fission) followed by congregational or denominational mergers, with consequent redundancy of buildings

■ Decline in chapel going

■ Matter-of-fact outlook: most of the free churches regard their buildings as 'special' only for as long they are in use for worship

Changes of site. You could try to find out how many nonconformist buildings existed in your area. Clues to former sites or their whereabouts may include:

Mike Corbishley

■ street names (for example 'Chapel Row', 'Zion Street')

■ converted buildings

■ entries in trades directories

■ nineteenth-century maps

■ old wedding photographs

■ denominational lists

■ local directories

■ memories of local people.

Do not overlook buildings you may have walked past many times, without recognising them for what they once were!

RIGHT: Ordnance Survey map of Bradford-on-Avon 1889.

PARKESTON QUAY, formed by the Great Eastern Railway Co. and opened for traffic in 1883, is si upon the Stour, 2½ miles up the river, and wa structed for developing their Continental traffic. quay, with station and loop line, occupied four ye construction, and cost about £500,000. Although a higher up the river than the old pier, there is a of time in starting from Parkeston quay, on acco the clearer course, and consequently the boat train London later than hitherto. About 600 acres of lan been acquired by the company, the greater porti claimed from the bed of the river, by a curved em ment 2½ miles long; in the centre of the curve quay, 1,800 feet long, affording berths for seven v while seven more can be moored in the river. The wall is formed by screw piles, those in front being in diameter, and those at the back being 1 foot between them are concrete cylinders of seven rings and 9 feet in outside diameter, sunk in pairs. On the quay are two goods warehouses, each 520 feet long by 100 feet wide. A passenger gangway 40 feet wide leads to the central building of 350 feet frontage, which serves for the station and hotel. All the buildings and platforms are erected upon piles, of which there are more than 1,000, sunk to the ancient bed of the river.

The church of St. Nicholas is a structure of white brick in the debased Perpendicular style, consisting of chancel nave, aisles and an embattled western tower, with pinnacles and spire, containing a clock and 8 bells: it was re built and enlarged in 1821 by subscription and a rate there are three partially-stained windows in the chancel and in the vestry is a tablet containing the names of th vicars of this church from 1336 to 1874: there are 1,500 sittings, of which 1,000 are free. The register date from the year 1550. The living is a vicarage, averag tithe rent-charge £45, net yearly value £51, in the gif of J. E. A. Gwynne esq. F.S.A. of Folkington manor Polegate, Sussex.

St. Nicholas Mission room, Bathside, erected in May 1879, is a wooden building, and will seat 40 persons.

There is an iron Mission church at Parkeston, seating about 100 persons.

The Catholic church, dedicated to our Lady of Mount Carmel, on the main road to Dovercourt, is a small edifice of brick in the Late Decorated style and was built from designs of E. Welby Pugin, in 1869: it has 100 sittings: the Rev. Robert Kelly is resident priest.

Here is a Baptist chapel, erected in 1821, with 250 seats; a Congregational chapel, built in 1800, and seating 200 persons; a Primitive Methodist chapel, buil with 200 sittings; a Wesleyan Methodist chape in 1829, and seating 500 adults and 60 child another Wesleyan chapel at Parkeston, erected with 260 sittings.

The burial ground of St. Nicholas parish, Dovercourt, covering an area of 5 acres, was 1855, and contains a mortuary chapel; it is control of a Burial Board of six members.

ABOVE: Extract from Kelly's Directory of Essex 1895.
RIGHT: Re-used non-conformist chapels.

Essex Archaeological Society

Wedding photograph of 1946 at Llanrhaidr-y-Mochnant chapel, North Wales.

Margaret Telford

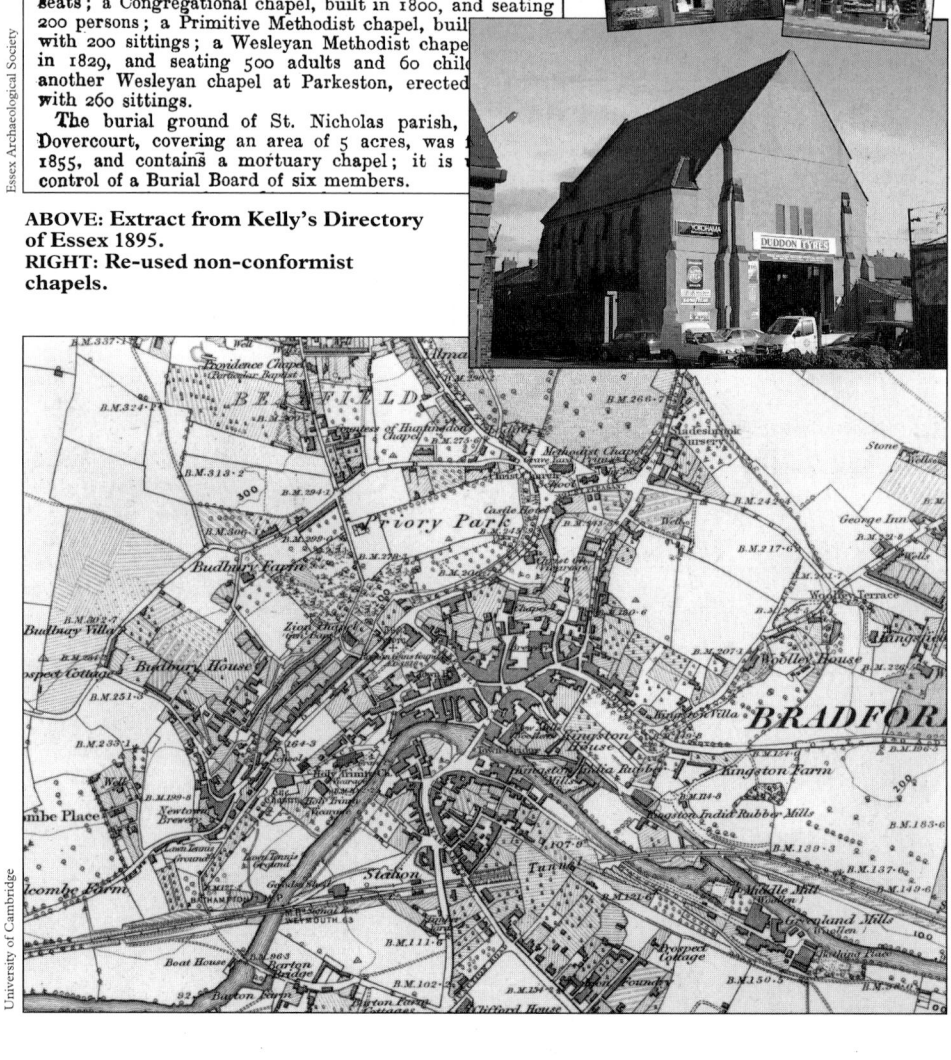

University of Cambridge

RECORDING

There are many opportunities for pupils to have opportunities to record church and chapel buildings and their associated memorials.

The building

Churches and chapels provide useful resources to practise measurement and drawing. You might also consider recording in other ways, such as photography or video.

Pupils can use angles to plan a building by using triangulation. Triangulation involves having three measurements in order to produce a triangle. One of these is a baseline, either a fixed feature such as a straight wall, or a line between two pegs as A - B in the drawing below. Point C is measured from each of the points A and B and drawn to scale using compasses.

The other method of drawing a ground plan is to use a similar base line and measure at right angles from it. In this drawing the base line is X - Y. Point Z is taken from a tape laid along the ground, measuring at right angles to a point on the church wall marked W.

A church wall can be drawn to scale using a simple clinometer.

Recording gravestones

About 20 million memorials are thought to exist in churchyards in Britain. Recording a complete graveyard is important because the gravestones themselves, and especially their inscriptions, provide us with a wealth of historical evidence - evidence which is fast disappearing through erosion, neglect and deliberate clearance of churchyards.

You could use proper Grave Memorial Recording Forms (information from the Council for British Archaeology, see page 36). On the back of this form (in use right) there is space to record the whole inscription and draw the memorial or fix a photograph.

RIGHT: A school churchyard project in Essex.

Recording graveyard memorials could include the methods of

■ making a plan of the location of all the tombstones

■ recording each memorial on a form

■ photographing each memorial.

After making the record, pupils will be able to analyse their data which will help them build up a picture of families and communities such as

Sequencing: All the graves in a churchyard can be collated into chronological order. Bear in mind that this sequence may contain gaps (stones may be missing), and that the positions of some stones may appear to be at odds with the sequence (for example, because stones have been moved from their original positions and re-erected).

Location: Were there parts of the churchyard developed at particular decades in the past? Where were the largest or most impressive graves located?

Family Trees: Do gravestones provide data to draw family trees? Can conclusions be drawn about family size in the past?

Names and occupations: Are their popular first names at particular periods? What occupations are represented?

Mike Corbishley

School with added classroom provision

Mike Corbishley

Here, it is easy to see that this twentieth-century house has been added to.

Mike Corbishley

This vestry was added to the building.

UNDERSTANDING

Looking at differences

Churches and cathedrals, and, to a lesser extent, chapels all show changes over time in the fabric of the building. Sometimes the change will have been made to accommodate a larger congregation. Sometimes it will be because the style of worship changed. You can prepare your pupils to understand evidence for change by priming them with examples of buildings with which they will be more familiar.

You will often see examples of extensions in schools - perhaps in your own.

You might then go on to look at church buildings to see the range of additions, or subtractions.

Then and now

If you can find an old illustration of a church building you could compare it, in detail, with what you can see today. This might be an exercise to carry out on site or you could use an example in the classroom. On site, you could ask pupils to record the differences by:

■ taking photographs

■ drawing sketches

■ making notes

■ recording on aural or video tape.

You may also find that the contrasting illustrations provide plenty of other discussion points - for example, people's clothes and the rural nature of a place in the last century.

How old is it?

Few churches are of a single date. Most were modified, modernised, enlarged or made smaller at different times. A typical church is an anthology of styles, with architectural contributions made at different times. Different styles can be used to unravel the sequence of the building. Rather like fashions in rock music or clothes, styles in medieval building were seldom static. Between about 1100 and 1500 forms of windows, doors, roofs, mouldings and masonry were

---

Case Study: St Paul's Church, Frizington, Cumbria.

Margaret Wiltshire, the Head Teacher of Frizington Primary School, decided to carry out a study of the parish church as part of a local history project with Year 5/6 pupils. This formed part of a joint project between English Heritage and the Department of Teaching and Educational Studies at Lancaster University. The aim was for the pupils to

■ become familiar with their parish church as part of a Victorian Britain topic: Frizington is an ex-mining village mostly built in the nineteenth century

■ increase awareness of the needs of visually-impaired people, especially pupils.

The pupils visited the church, interviewed the vicar and the verger and researched the history of the building. They then spent some time working with a tutor and students from Lancaster University learning about visual impairment and how it affects

Andrew White

people's lives. Back at the church the pupils, now in groups, focused on different aspects of the church to investigate how they could make it more accessible to visually impaired people. The pupils:

■ created tactile material such as tiles from clay, art straws, wood and wire

■ recreated walls using clay

■ made a tactile floor plan

■ created a large print guide book and audio cassette guide.

Finally the pupils were able to evaluate their own work when they invited a group of pupils from the Royal National Institute for the Blind at New College, Worcester to visit their church.

Council for British Archaeology

Successive interruption of one feature by another in the church at Avebury, Wiltshire.

ABOVE and BELOW: Ramsey church, Essex. The drawing was made in 1851; the photograph was taken in 1996.

of a building were erected. For example, if a window has been pierced through a wall, then the wall must be earlier than the window. This kind of relationship is called relative chronology. Archaeologists produce matrix diagrams - flow diagrams - to record the relationships of excavated features or sets of building activity in upstanding structures.

You could construct a relatively easy exercise for you pupils using a local parish church. The best way of recording is to make a sketch of the wall, number or letter the individual features and then use the architectural features illustration to produce a flow chart. The example below is taken from the church at Wroxeter, Shropshire (see also page 23).

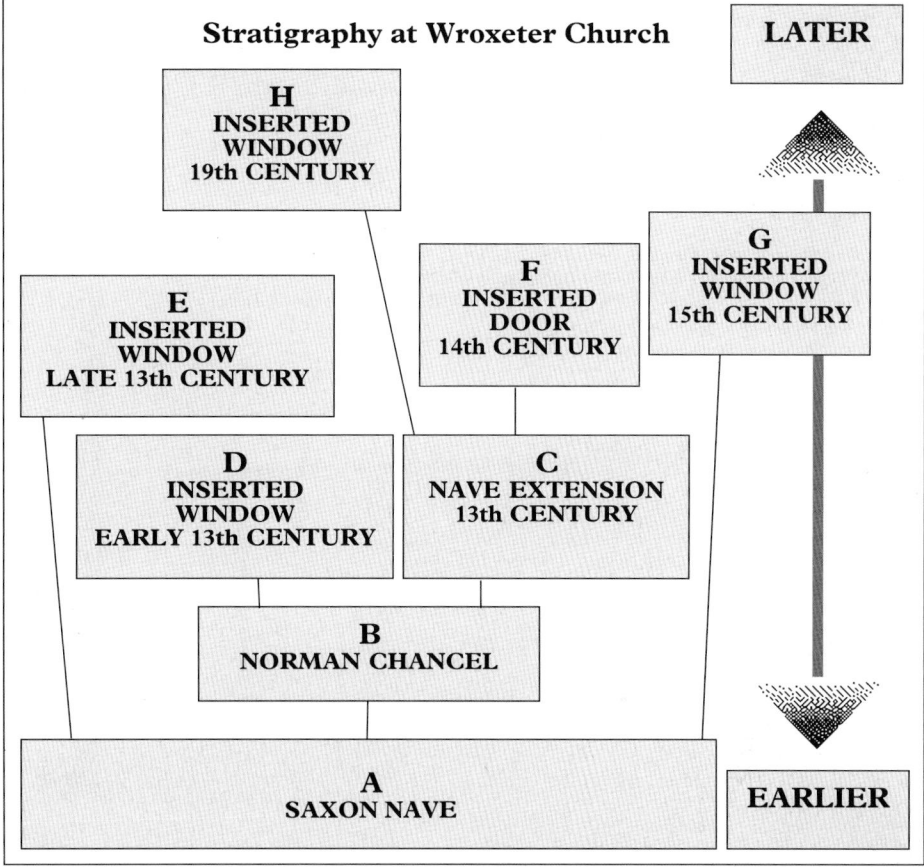

Stratigraphy at Wroxeter Church

LATER

H INSERTED WINDOW 19th CENTURY

E INSERTED WINDOW LATE 13th CENTURY

F INSERTED DOOR 14th CENTURY

G INSERTED WINDOW 15th CENTURY

D INSERTED WINDOW EARLY 13th CENTURY

C NAVE EXTENSION 13th CENTURY

B NORMAN CHANCEL

A SAXON NAVE

EARLIER

almost always in a state of change. Nineteenth-century antiquaries classified these styles, providing a system of names and dating of the Norman and several Gothic styles which we still use today.

The nineteenth century was the second great age of church building, when architects tended either to recollect medieval styles in a kind of free paraphrase, or else to imitate them directly - the Gothic revival.

Don't be put off by confusing stylistic labels or technical jargon. A pupil does not need to remember whether Perpendicular comes before or after Early English, or to know what tracery is, in order to see that a traceried window differs from a window with no tracery at all. The essential things to look for are differences and contrasts, and then to sort different stages of work into a logical sequence.

This introduces principles of phasing, and methods of dating - processes which are basic to archaeological excavation, as well as the analysis of buildings.

Phasing simply means sorting out the order in which different parts

ABOVE: Recording the stratigraphy of Wroxeter church in matrix form.

RIGHT: Wroxeter church, Shropshire, a view from the north showing the features of the building analysed in the above matrix.

BELOW: Drawing of the north wall of Wroxeter church showing the succession of building alterations from A to H as displayed in the matrix diagram above.

How were buildings used?

One method of using the physical evidence to work out how a building might have been used is to present plans to pupils. Below are a series of simplified plans from a range of buildings, from the familiar (a 'typical' house) to the more difficult (law court) to church buildings. You could photocopy (at a larger size) these drawings for use in class. You can then ask the pupils:

■ to look carefully at the scale of each building

■ to see if it is domestic or public

■ to see whether the fixtures and fittings help work out what each room or space might have been used for

■ to find a focus to each building, if there is one

■ to find evidence for the routes people might have taken inside or around each building

■ to reach a conclusion about the type of building giving reasons based only on the evidence in the plans.

There will be obvious discussion points especially with reference to the plans of the cinema, church and chapel. For example:

■ the cinema has aisles but is this for the audience to reach the stage?

■ the church has a central aisle which reflects the religious practice in parish churches

but

■ as there is no requirement for a processional aisle in nonconformists buildings, the centre of the floor is filled with pews.

RIGHT: Modern detached house, ground floor plan. A: front door and hall; B: garage; C: lavatory; D: kitchen; E: utility room ?
F and G: dining room and lounge - which is most likely to be which ?

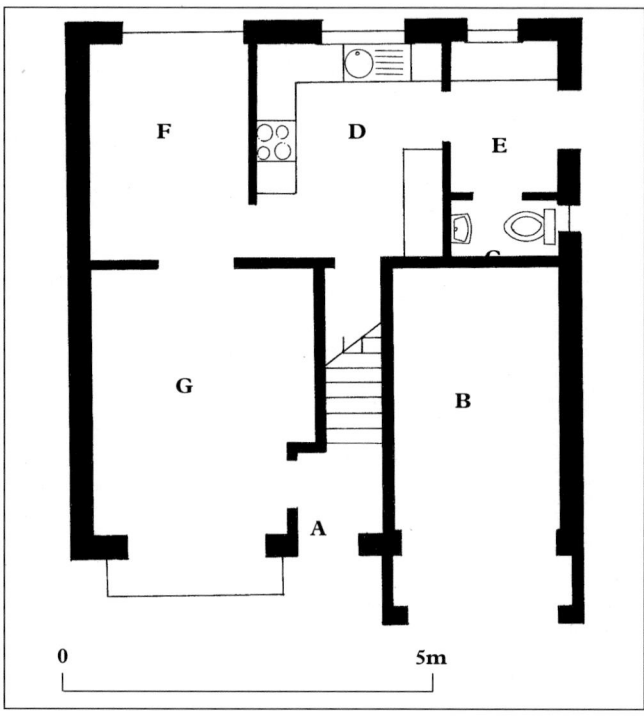

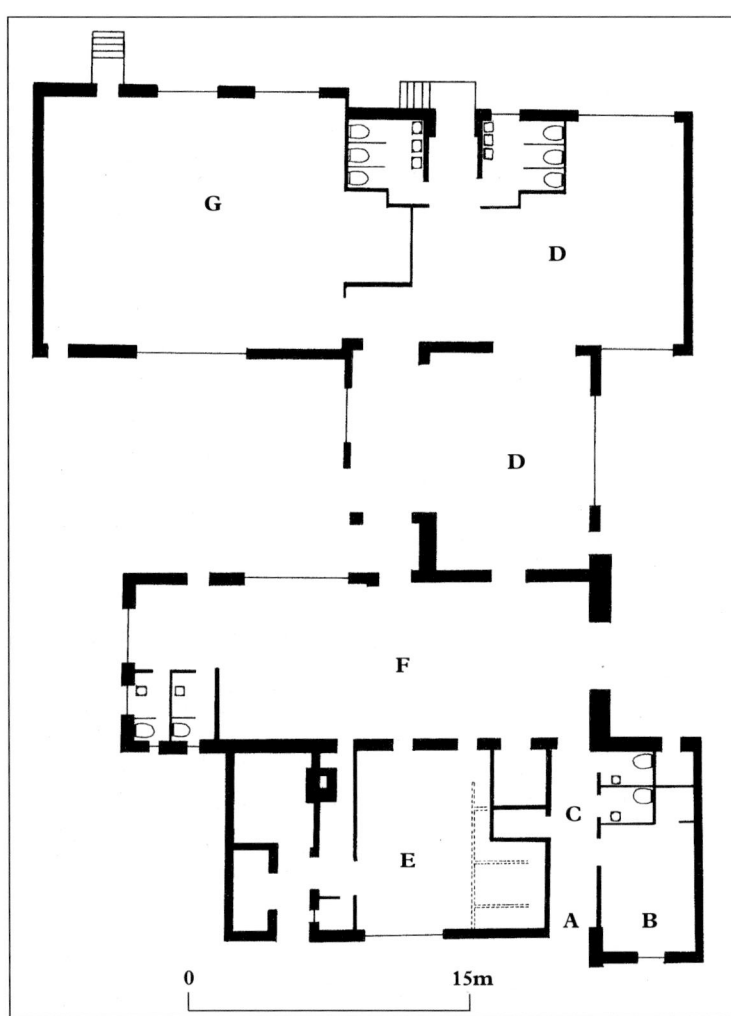

ABOVE: Modern primary school, built on one level.

A: main entrance
B: office
C: staff toilets
D: classrooms
E: kitchen, stores and boiler room
F: open dining hall
G: hall

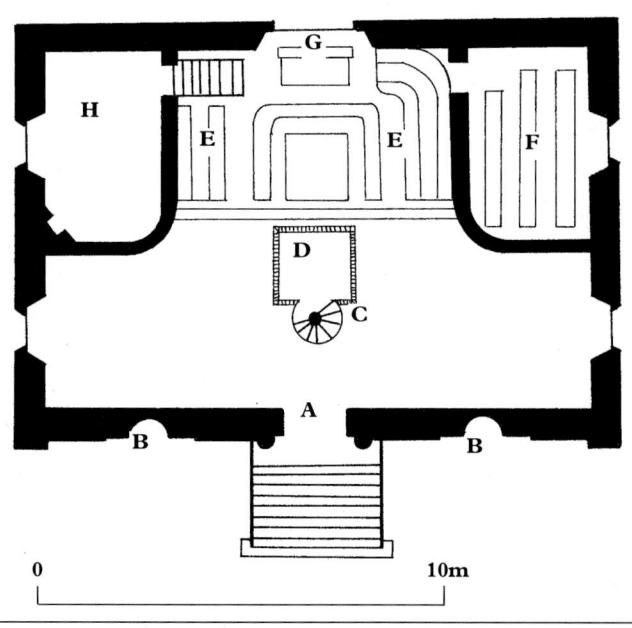

RIGHT: Law court, based on the 1818 design for the court house at Ballyconnell, Co Cavan.

A: entrance; B: niches for statues
C: spiral stairs to prisoners' cells
D: dock
E; seating for lawyers and court staff
F: seating for jury
G: judge's bench
H: judge's chamber

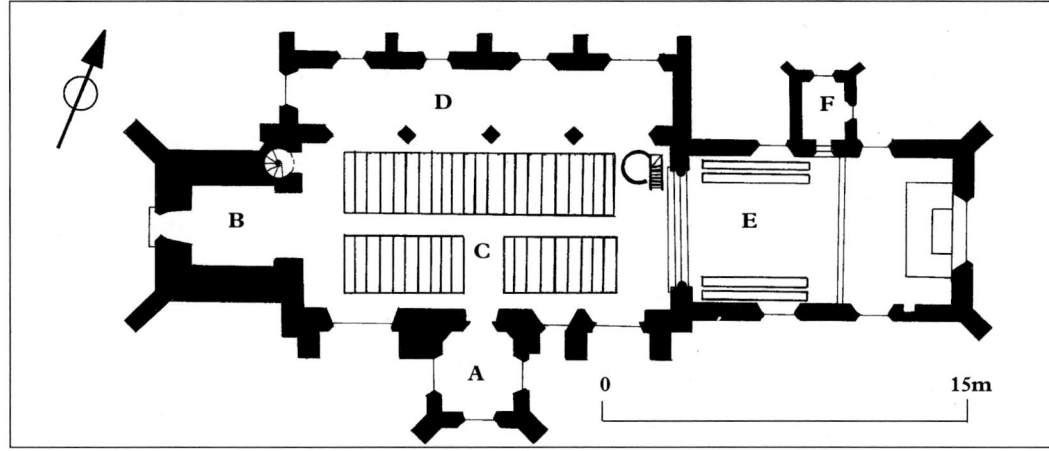

LEFT: Parish church, based on All Saints, Feering in Essex, with a fourteenth-century north aisle to the nave and a fifteenth-century bell tower.

A: entrance and porch
B: tower
C: nave
D: aisle
E: chancel
F: vestry

0   15m

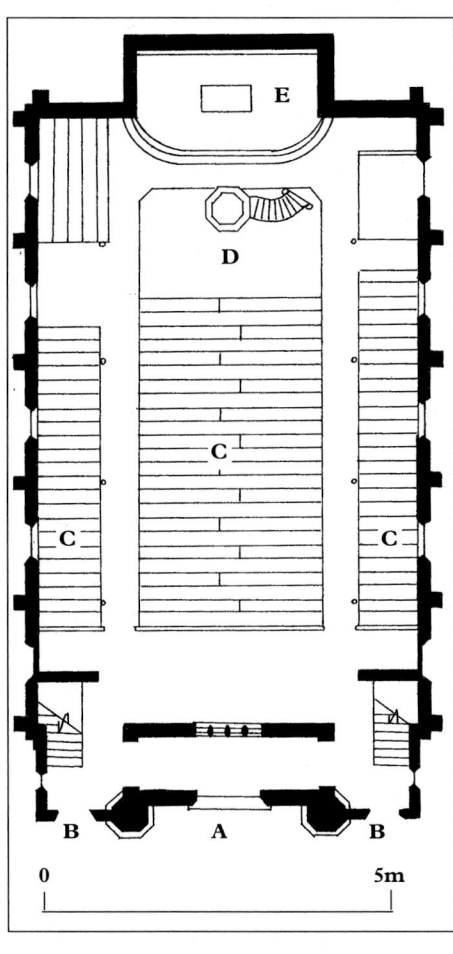

ABOVE: Nonconformist chapel, based on the Wesleyan Methodist Chapel, Newbury, Berkshire, built in 1837.

A: main entrance
B: side entrances to access gallery
C: seating
D: pulpit
E: table

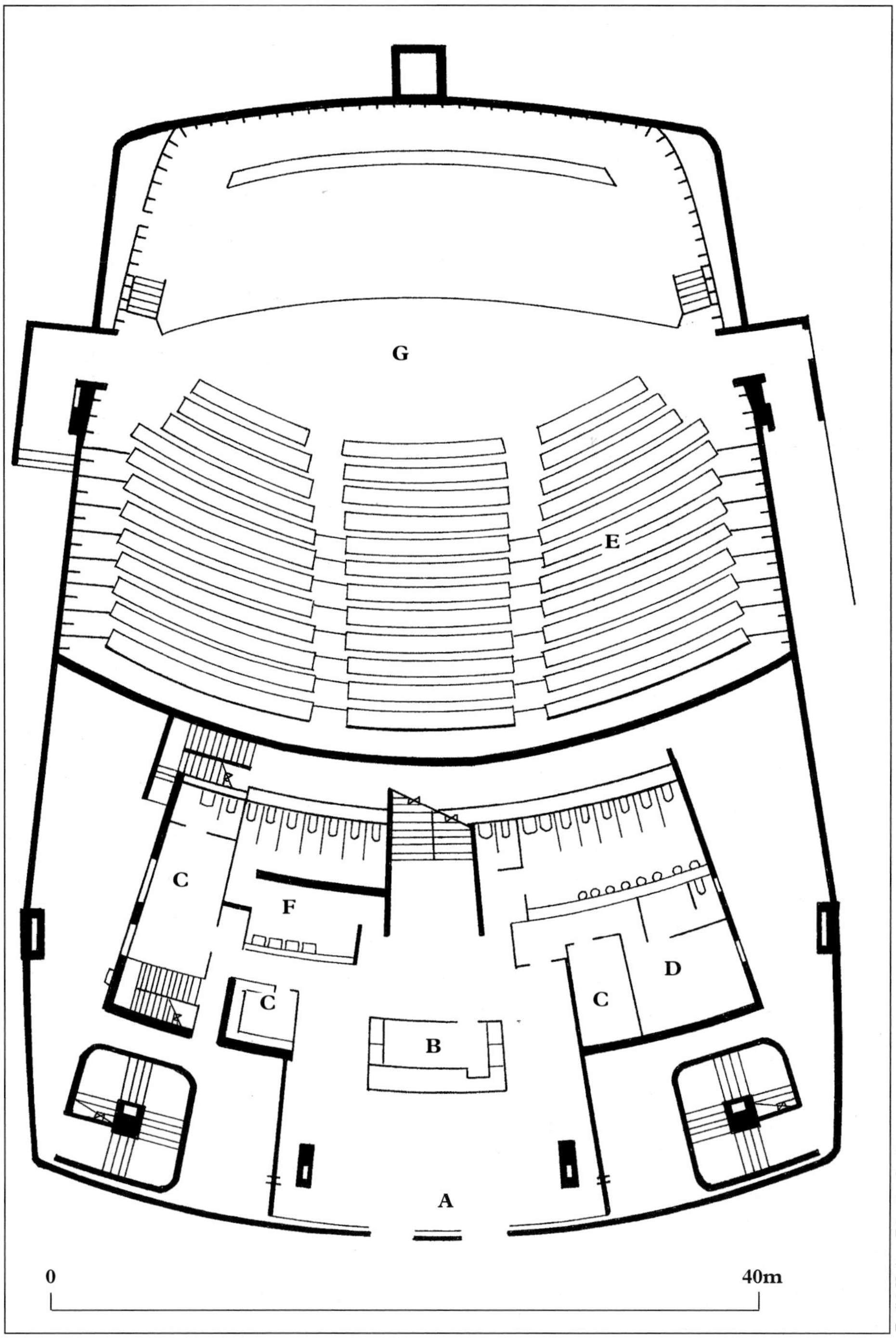

RIGHT: Cinema, based on the Odeon, Elephant and Castle, London, built in 1966.

A: entrance and foyer
B: ticket office
C: staff rooms
D: manager's office
E: men's lavatories
F: powder room and women's lavatories
G: auditorium and screen

0   40m

English Heritage Education Service

CHURCHES ACROSS THE CURRICULUM

Churches, cathedrals and chapels can be used to bring together a number of different curriculum areas.

ENGLISH

Pupils will be able to increase their knowledge about language, for example by using modern guides to churches and comparing that type of writing with both tourist guides for other places to visit and reports and guides from, say, earlier in this century.

MATHS

There are a number of different elements which are fundamental to the maths curriculum which can be found in buildings, but perhaps especially in church buildings. You might consider:

■ shape, through ground plans; design, through windows and doors

■ measurement, through making drawings of individual features or the whole building.

SCIENCE

You could examine and research the different methods church builders used in the past. Lime mortar, which is still used today, was produced by adding water to quicklime (calcium oxide) and sand. The water and lime combined to produce calcium hydroxide (hydrated lime), which then set as the surplus water was lost by evaporation.

Rural churchyards are often important havens for plant and insect communities. Botanical surveys offer projects which can be both instructive and practically beneficial - for example, results can be used to help devise a management plan for the churchyard.

The church itself may provide nesting and roosting sites for birds (for example, swallows, martins and owls) and many churches contain bat roosts.

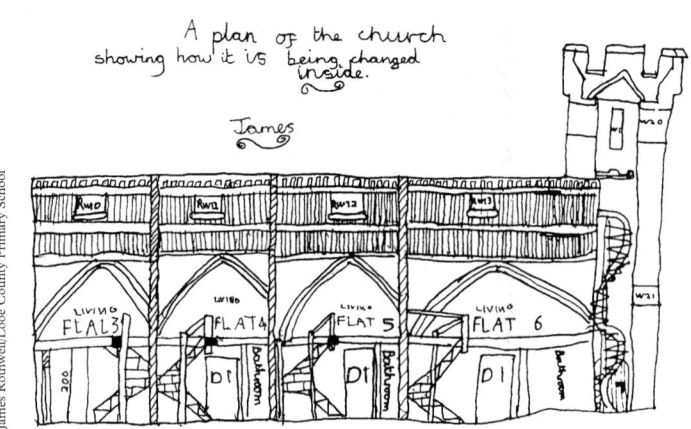

A plan of the church showing how it is being changed inside.

James

James Rothwell/Looe County Primary School

LEFT: A drawing of a redundant church, by a primary school pupil, showing how it is being converted into flats.

HISTORY

At Key Stage 1, churches will usually provide an easy access to an old, or even ancient, building which will have many connections with older people in the community, through oral history, documents and photographs. The church will often be the ideal starting point for a local history project at Key Stage 2 and one in which you can demonstrate to parents and governors a real connection with the local community.

GEOGRAPHY

The location of a church can form a central part of work in geography, especially for mapping skills. You might also consider the question of how materials were brought to churches in the medieval period when water was the preferred medium for bulk carriage. As a rule of thumb, costs of land transport began to exceed the costs of materials themselves above a distance of 12 miles. You might investigate, for example:

■ what the components of churches (large timbers, for instance) tell us about the more remote elements of the medieval communications system

■ whether there are any materials (for instance, stone brought from afar) which reflect canal and railway building in the eighteenth and nineteenth centuries

DESIGN AND TECHNOLOGY

Churches and cathedrals offer an excellent introduction to issues of structural engineering. You can investigate how forces and thrusts behave, for example, and the structural principles of arches and vaults.

ART

A church will provide all the visual elements you need to give pupils first-hand experiences in art, for example, pattern, texture, tone and shape.

RELIGIOUS EDUCATION

Specific suggestions are made in the Model Syllabuses for incorporating a visit to a local church, which may be part of your own school's syllabus. However, you might also consider a number of other issues, for example:

■ the closure or re-use of many chapels in recent times (see page 28)

■ the adaptation of existing churches or chapels for use by other religions, for instance by Hindus or Muslims

■ the existence of purpose-made buildings for non-Christian faiths, for instance synagogues.

RESOURCES AND BIBLIOGRAPHY

BOOKS FOR TEACHERS

Churches
Chatfield, M, **Churches the Victorians forgot**, Moorland Publishing, 1989. Evocative, illustrated tour of some buildings which escaped nineteenth-century restoration.

Child, M, **Discovering Church Architecture**, Shire, 1991, ISBN 0-85263-328-9.

Clarke, B F L, **Church builders of the nineteenth century**, David & Charles, 1969, ISBN 0-7153-5141-9

Curl, J, Stevens, **Victorian Churches**, Batsford/English Heritage, 1995, ISBN 0-7134-7491-2.

Friar, S, **A companion to the English Parish Church**, Alan Sutton, 1996, ISBN 0-7509-0461-5

Morris, R, **Churches in the landscape**, Dent, 1989, ISBN 0-460-86014-3

Needham, A, **How to study an old church**, Batsford, 1944. Out of print but buy a copy if you see one. It is full of clear drawings.

Rodwell, W, **Church Archaeology**, Batsford/English Heritage, 1989, ISBN 0-7134-6294-9. Well-illustrated, lively and as yet unsurpassed introduction to church archaeology.

Cathedrals
Harvey, J H, **Cathedrals of England and Wales**, Batsford, 1974, ISBN 0-7134-0616-X.

Tatton-Brown, T, **Great Cathedrals of Britain**, BBC Books, 1989, ISBN 0-563-20730-2.

Wilson, C, **The Gothic Cathedral: the Architecture of the Great Church 1130-1530**, Thames & Hudson, 1990, ISBN 0-500-34105-2.

Chapels and meeting houses
Barton, D a, **Discovering Chapels and Meeting Houses**, Shire, 1990, ISBN 0-7478-0097-9.

Materials
Clifton-Taylor, A, **The pattern of English building**, Faber, 1972, ISBN 0-571-09525-9.

Investigation and recording
Arnold, H G et al, **Hallelujah! Recording chapels and meeting houses**, Council for British Archaeology, 1985, ISBN 0-906780-49-7. Introductory guide to the history, diversity and study of nonconformist buildings.

Braithwaite, L, **Exploring British Cities**, a & C Black, 1986, ISBN 0-7136-2748-4. A useful guide, illustrated with nineteenth-century maps, to a range of buildings including churches, cathedrals and chapels.

Cameron, K, **English Place Names**, Batsford, 1996, ISBN 0-7134-7378-9. Up-dated classic reference work on the interpretation of place names.

Cocke, T et al, **Recording a church: an illustrated glossary, Council for British Archaeology Practical Handbook 7**, 1996, ISBN 1-872414-56-7. Extremely useful, inexpensive and reliable guide to the anatomy and features of parish churches.

Parsons, D, **Churches and chapels: investigating places of worship**, Council for British Archaeology Practical Handbook 8, 1989, ISBN 0-906780-86-1. Compact introduction to the study of churches and chapels. Advice on first steps in recording.

Churchyards and tombstone recording
Burgess, F, **English Churchyard Memorials**, Lutterworth Press, 1963. The most authoritative book on churchyard memorials.

Burman, P & Stapleton, H, **The Churchyards Handbook: Advice on the history and significance of churchyards, their care, improvement and maintenance**, Church House Publishing, 1988, ISBN 0-7151-7554-8. An invaluable guide.

Child, M, **Discovering Churchyards**, Shire, 1989, ISBN 0-85263-6.

Jones, J, **How to record graveyards**, Council for British Archaeology/RESCUE, 1984, ISBN 0-906780-43-8. Introduction to the why and how of studying and recording graveyards.

BOOKS FOR PUPILS
Corbishley, M, **The Middle Ages**, Facts on File, 1990, ISBN 0-8160-1973-8. With a section on the medieval church and cathedral building.

Fewins, C, **Be a Church Detective: a Young Person's Guide to Old Churches**, The National Society and Church House Publishing, 1992, ISBN 0-7151-4790-0. An excellent introductory guide for pupils.

Macaulay, D, **Cathedral: The Story of Its Construction**, Collins, 1974, ISBN 0-00-192150-9.

Macdonald, F & James, J, **A Medieval Cathedral**, Simon & Schuster, 1991, ISBN 0-7500-0787-7.

Pluckrose, H, **Local History Detective: Churches**, Simon & Schuster, 1993, ISBN 0-7501-0450-3.

TEACHING STRATEGIES
Books in the English Heritage Education on Site teacher's guide series which have specific sections on or particular reference to churches:

Barnicoat, J, **Newspapers and Education**, English Heritage, 1994, ISBN 1-85074-511-0.

Cooksey, C, **Using Abbeys**, English Heritage, 1992, ISBN 1-85074-328-2.

Copeland, T, **Maths and the Historic Environment**, English Heritage, 1992, ISBN 1-85074-329-0.

Copeland, T, **Geography and the historic environment**, English Heritage, 1993, ISBN 1-85074-332-0.

David, R, **History at Home**, English Heritage, 1996, ISBN 1-85074-591-9.

Davies, I and Webb, C, **Using Documents**, English Heritage, 1996, ISBN 1-85074-478-5.

Moffat, H, and Neave, D, **Looking at Buildings - The East Riding**, English Heritage/Penguin Books, 1995, ISBN 0140-710-647.

Pownall, J and Hudson, N, **Science and the historic environment**, English Heritage, 1992, ISBN 1-85074-331-2.

Purkis, S, **Using Memorials**, English Heritage, 1995, ISBN 1-85074-493-9.

Videos

Videos in English Heritage's Frameworks of Worship series touch many of the themes in this book. The series introduces different aspects of the historical development of churches and considers some of the ways in which archaeologists gather and use information. Suitability begins with Key Stage 4, but teachers of younger pupils will find them rewarding.

In Memoriam: the archaeology of graveyards, English Heritage, 1990, 21 minutes. Links between ecology, archaeology, art and social history are explored in a video which suggests how a churchyard or cemetery may be used as an outdoor classroom.

Buildings and Beliefs, English Heritage, 20 minutes. An exploration of the relationship between form and function, structure and spirituality.

The Master Builders: the construction of a great church, English Heritage, 1991, 23 minutes. Introduction to issues of construction and technology of Beverley Minster.

Chapels: the buildings of nonconformity, English Heritage, 1989, 18 minutes. Introduction to the diversity and functional characteristics of nonconformist architecture.

Gods Acre: nature conservation in the churchyard, English Heritage, 1993, 24 minutes. Explores the relationship between churchyards as cultural sites and ecology, and introduces some management techniques for nature conservation in rural churchyards.

Cathedral Archaeology, English Heritage, 1996, 21 minutes. Investigates the ways archaeologists record and excavate evidence in cathedrals, using Canterbury and Norwich as case studies.

LOCAL SOURCES

Reference library

Here you may find regional and local studies, monographs on some individual buildings, publications to do with context (for example histories of particular towns, the industrial revolution), journals of local and county historical, archaeological and record societies contain a wealth of information.

County Record Office

For primary sources such as written records and historic maps, the Record Office is an invaluable source. Most offices publish leaflets which explain what their collections contain, and how they may be consulted. Within or linked to the CRO may also be the Diocesan Archive, which will contain many parish records, including faculties (licences) for alterations and rebuilding. Many cathedrals have their own libraries.

Sites and Monuments Record (SMR)

The SMR is a database for the historic environment. Used chiefly for planning purposes, it is also an educational tool - and may contain a large collection of aerial photographs. SMRs are mostly located at county level, but some are based upon districts or towns.

The Council for British Archaeology's concern for the archaeological study of churches is reflected in a lengthy list of publications. Advice on how to get started is available from the CBA's Education Officer, who may put you in touch with one of the honorary Education Liaison Officers who operate in each CBA Region. The Council for British Archaeology can recommend other contacts and resources, and put you in touch with your local SMR or archaeological society. A list of publications (including a number of church excavation reports) is available free on request.

Education Officer
CBA
Bowes Morrell House
111 Walmgate
York YO1 2UA
Tel: 0904 671417
Fax: 01904 671384
e-mail: 100 271.456 @ compuserve.com

For a detailed list of organisations concerned with churches, cathedrals and chapels please contact either English Heritage Education Service or the Council for British Archaeology at the addresses on this page.

Acknowledgements
The authors would like to thank the following people for help with this book: Mick Sharp for providing some of the photographs, Lewis Braithwaite for providing prints of nineteenth century maps, the Essex Archaeological Society for allowing the use of the Kelly's Directory of Essex, the Essex Record Office for permission to use the estate map of Aldham, Dick and Marjorie Richards for locating a family wedding photograph and Purcell Miller Tritton and Partners for providing the photograph of St Andrew's Church, Eaton, the Reverend Stanley Smith.

OPPOSITE: Advertisement from Kelly's Directory of Essex, 1895. (Essex Archaeological Society)